MANAGING PROFESSIONAL DEVELOPMENT IN EDUCATION

MANAGING PROFESSIONAL DEVELOPMENT IN EDUCATION

Issues in Policy and Practice

Derek Glover and Sue Law

RoutledgeFalmer
Taylor & Francis Group

LONDON AND NEW YORK

First published in 1996
By Kogan Page Limited

Reprinted 2004
By RoutledgeFalmer,
2 Park Square, Milton Park, Abingdon, Oxon, OX14 4RN

Transferred to Digital Printing 2004

British Library Cataloguing in Publication Data

CIP record for this book is available from the British Library.

ISBN 0 7494 1989 X

Typeset by Kogan Page

Contents

Abbreviations and Acronyms

ACSET	Advisory Committee on the Supply and Education of Teachers
ACSTT	Advisory Committee on the Supply and Training of Teachers
CPD	Continuing Professional Development
DES	Department of Education and Science
DfE	Department for Education
DfEE	Department for Education and Employment
DoE	Department of Employment
ERA	Education Reform Act
ESG	Education Support Grant
FE	Further Education
FEFC	Further Education Funding Council
GCSE	General Certificate of Secondary Education
GEST	Grant for Education Support and Training
GMS	Grant Maintained School
GRIDS	Guidelines for Review and Internal Development in Schools
HEADLAMP	Headteachers' Leadership and Administration Programme
HEFC(E)	Higher Education Funding Council (England)
HEFC(W)	Higher Education Funding Council (Wales)
HEI	Higher Education Institution
HOD	Head of Department
IDP	Institutional Development Plan
INSET	Inservice Education and Training
ITE	Initial Teacher Education
ITT	Initial Teacher Training
KEEP	Keele Effective Educators Project
LEA	Local Education Authority
LEATGS	Local Education Authority Training Grant Scheme

LMS	Local Management of Schools
MCI	Management Charter Initiative
NCE	National Commission on Education
NQT	Newly Qualified Teacher
NVQ	National Vocational Qualification
OFSTED	Office for Standards in Education
PDC	Professional Development Coordinator
PDP	Personal Development Plan
PGCE	Postgraduate Certificate of Education
PTA	Parent–Teacher Association
RoA	Record of Achievement
SD	Staff Development
SDC	Staff Development Coordinator
SDP	School Development Plan
SEFC	Scottish Education Funding Council
SEN	Special Educational Needs
SHEFC	Scottish Higher Education Funding Council
SMTF	School Management Task Force
SPG	Special Purposes Grant
TTA	Teachers' Training Agency
TVEI	Technical and Vocational Education Initiative

Acknowledgements

We should like to acknowledge the support and generosity of time given by the staff of the very many primary and secondary schools who, since 1993, have supported our research. They have produced extensive commentaries on their professional development policies and practices, as well as provided us with a significant amount of factual data. Our thanks are also due to the group of secondary schools who have become involved in the Keele Effective Educators Project (KEEP) and the many staff who have given their time to attend meetings, undertake interviews and complete extensive questionnaires as part of our case study work. We look forward to the next stage of our work with them. Barry Pitt also deserves thanks for his work in compiling case study data in two KEEP schools. Lastly, and most importantly, we should like to thank Celia and Mark Glover and David, Katie and Daniel Law for maintaining the momentum of family life while we endeavoured to maintain the momentum of writing.

Introduction

Professional development has been undergoing a quiet revolution. Over the past decade we have been witnessing what amounts to an overhaul of structures and relationships in the continuing professional development of teachers in England and Wales. A decade ago it was possible for individuals to gain significant support for long-term secondment and for Local Education Authorities (LEAs) to structure the training and development activities of all their schools as part of an overall corporate paternalism. Ten years later, short-term training and development is often school-based, and increasing numbers of teachers self-fund their own long-term professional development.

During the 1980s, the nature of continuing professional development (CPD) and inservice education and training (INSET) varied widely between LEAs. For the most part, however, provision was frequently based on top-down needs identification; was often offered in support of government funded and directed initiatives like the Low Attainers Project (LAP), or the introduction of General Certificate of Secondary Education (GCSE); was driven by LEA 'training menus'; was characterized by individualized and sometimes muddled approaches to planning; was often used to support individual career development initiatives; and had little or nothing to do with evaluation or issues of effectiveness and value for money. In essence, continuing professional development rarely consisted of coherent and planned schemes aimed at *all* teachers within the context of overall institutional growth.

The late 1980s brought a sea-change in educational policy and practice which effectively swept professional development along in its wake. The structures of INSET became more organized during the 1980s – especially after Circular 6/86 which introduced a new funding scheme, changes to schoolteachers' pay and conditions in 1987, and appraisal and specified training days. However, it was the 1988 Education Reform Act which proved the major catalyst for change. The 1990s has seen the development of a more

1

autonomous schools system and the establishment of 'site-based school management' with a linked focus on institutional accountability. In effect, there has been a government-driven push towards greater school-centredness – but, importantly, within a framework of greater government-directedness.

As a consequence of this general thrust, professional development has also become increasingly school-based, enabling the establishment of more for-malized institutional responses to development demands within the new embryonic education market. Schools and colleges working within the new infrastructure and relationships are, however, now subject to greater public scrutiny of their performance through the Office for Standards in Education (OFSTED) inspection process and via the publication of 'league tables' showing annual public examination results for individual schools. In Chapter 1, we further outline the historical evolution of policy and practice and the general background to the present management and organization of continu-ing professional development as one aspect of an evolving national education system.

Defining CPD

These changes, together with the establishment of national guidelines on inservice education and training as part of teachers' new conditions of service, have led increasingly to more whole-school and college attempts to evolve coherent programmes of institutionally driven activities, variously known as 'CPD', 'INSET', 'teacher development' and 'staff development'. There has been much debate over specific definitions of these various terms (eg, Dean, 1993; O'Sullivan *et al.*, 1988) and no single and agreed definition exists. The rapidly changing nature of development practice and process has undoubtedly influenced both the meaning and use of these terms. While there are difficul-ties surrounding the precise nature of the various definitions, this book, in line with common practice elsewhere (eg, Fullan, 1992) uses the terms INSET, CPD, teacher development and staff development interchangeably (for further discussion see Chapter 2).

Bolam's conception of CPD offers a useful working definition here (Bolam, 1982a; 1993), since it incorporates the concepts of education, training and support within a portfolio of activities engaged in by teachers and educa-tion managers following on from initial teacher certification with the aims of:

- adding to their professional knowledge;
- improving their professional skills;
- clarifying their professional values; and
- enabling their students to be educated more effectively.

2

Bolam's definition assumes that, in essence, CPD embodies three components:

1. *professional training:* short courses, conferences and workshops, largely focused on practice and skills;
2. *professional education:* longer courses and/or secondments, focused on theory and research-based knowledge; and
3. *professional support:* job-embedded arrangements/procedures.

Researching CPD

Three years ago the Inservice Education and Management Unit (IEMU) at Keele University initiated survey-based research with the aim of establishing an INSET database to record changes in professional development management and practices in England and Wales. Since 1993, annual questionnaire surveys have been conducted on a national basis, providing responses from between 40 and 50 primary and 50 and 60 secondary schools across ten different LEAs each year and using a balance of rural, semi-rural and urban schools. Annual research update reports have been published on the basis of the data gathered and conclusions drawn. Approximately one-fifth of the responding secondary and one-tenth of the primary schools have been grant-maintained schools working with different funding arrangements and, consequently, providing some differences in response.

During 1995, the Keele Effective Educators Project (KEEP) was initiated with the aim of fostering action research with partner schools, using 'critical friend' CPD support integrated within a variety of school improvement projects. During the planning stages of the project two one-day HEI-school conferences provided a valuable information base on the CPD policy issues being encountered. Fieldwork comprising semi-structured interviews, further individual staff questionnaires and access to documentary evidence (eg, inspection reports) was subsequently carried out in 12 comprehensive schools (three of which were grant-maintained) distributed across six LEAs. The focus is on identifying the nature of policy-making, CPD organization and impact within each institution across all staffing levels. Information deriving from survey information in addition to fieldwork in project schools forms much of the basis of the material in Chapter 2, which examines how the changes in the structuring and management of CPD has influenced its organization within schools.

Annual professional development surveys have indicated marked changes in the way that professional development opportunities are provided. For example, OFSTED's reorganization of inspection has influenced dramatically the nature of advisory and inspectoral roles within LEAs and, at the same time, helped provoke the establishment of more comprehensive consultancy work within the higher education sector as well as the burgeoning private consultancy market. Schools have now been placed very much at the centre – as 'clients' and 'customers' in the new INSET marketplace. Ironically, however, schools are faced with a plethora of service providers and opportunities at a time of diminishing resources and a growing imperative to search out value for money. These and other issues concerning the management of professional development supply and the demand for quality services form the basis of analysis in Chapter 3.

As part of our investigations, an examination of a series of OFSTED reports was undertaken: 100 of the secondary reports produced during 1994/5 were analysed in detail in order to provide an overview and examples of both commended and criticized professional development practice within schools. We have identified a general pattern of support within OFSTED reports for those schools whose professional development planning and implementation strategies grow out of school development planning, and of less favourable comment where this link is not maintained or where appraisal is inadequate or not used as a starting point for planning individual development opportunities. OFSTED reports also stress the importance of the evaluation of CPD and the need for a continuing assessment of the impact which CPD has on the quality of teaching and learning within institutions. This focus has also contributed to the interpretation of practice and selection of examples used from case-study evidence in Chapter 4.

As part of our survey development, we simultaneously collected a series of open-ended commentaries from respondents indicating the perceived impact of professional development and its organization on classroom and management practice, as well as its perceived influence over teaching and learning and the institutional life of schools. Open commentaries have also provided information on the kinds of tensions which schools have been experiencing as part of increasing institutional autonomy on the one hand, and greater accountability on the other. These developments have also been characterized by a growing awareness amongst senior managers of the increasing professional expectations amongst teachers, much of which has followed on from the introduction of appraisal at a time of generally static or declining resources. The impact of these policy issues is considered in particular in Chapter 5, where we review staff perceptions of INSET opportunities, including views on the costs and benefits identified by these stakeholders.

Data from interviews involving 60 members of staff in a cross-section of roles (from headteacher, deputy head, professional development coordinator, head of department/year, to mainscale teacher/newly qualified teacher) across the 12 partnership schools forms a significant element in the development of the case studies in Chapter 6, in which three of the twelve case studies compiled are provided with a commentary which suggests that schools are progressing at different rates along a continuum towards establishing effective and coherent CPD systems. In certain respects, therefore, this report on research may appear premature because action research projects are taking place during 1996/7 and may provide evidence of more sophisticated and effective CPD management within a whole institutional environment. Each KEEP project has modest financial support, raising the issue of the importance of 'honey pot' funding as a catalyst for development. The planned activities so far identified with schools indicate that schools are potentially rich sources of development opportunity and illustrate the value of relatively simple development strategies like work-shadowing, paired observations and mentoring. Our analysis of OFSTED reports also supports this contention.

In addition to interviews within KEEP case study schools, further questionnaires were completed by 75 members of staff in case study schools – from headteachers to newly qualified teachers. These questionnaires focus predominantly on the ways in which individual staff have been affected by the organization and availability of INSET opportunities during their careers and, in particular, over recent years. Questionnaires also sought views on the allocation of resources and the effect of professional development on individual and whole-school development. This material, backed by field study interviews and notes of discussion at KEEP day conferences, has been helpful in establishing the descriptors of various cultural backdrops which enhance or inhibit teacher development. Chapter 7 utilizes this material extensively in presenting a possible model of an effective professional development culture, as well as informing suggestions concerning good practice throughout the text.

Towards Teacher Effectiveness

In many ways there has been a great expansion of professional development opportunities over the past decade as well as a growing awareness that schools are potentially fertile ground for improvement – for encouraging the growth of knowledge, the command of skills, or a change in attitudes amongst staff as well as students. Throughout this project evidence has been gathered of the ways in which various organizations within significantly different environments are approaching training and development issues. Some begin with the stance that all aspects of human resource management provide opportunities for professional growth. Others take a more instrumental view that 'when a skill is needed then we train for it'. There is, in addition, a range of perceptions between the two ends of the spectrum.

Whatever their philosophical approach, KEEP partner schools have provided a considerable body of evidence on their planning, delivery, monitoring and evaluation strategies. Examples of the evidence gathered over three years are provided within the body of the text. In addition, in the belief that we should try to demonstrate a wider conception of 'development' and in order to provide a more interactive text, readers are offered opportunities at various points to reflect on their own personal experiences, attitudes and practices. We hope that such opportunities will enable groups of practitioners to examine their own practice with more deliberation and structure. In this respect, we also hope we are promoting the link between whole-school or college development and the effective management of staff through rational professional development planning, while maintaining room for personal professional development.

In writing this book we have been aware that important development work is being undertaken elsewhere in the world – in North America, Oceania and on mainland Europe for example – and that there is a growing need for greater interactivity between each of these arenas in the dissemination of good practice and research outcomes. It is essential, for example, that the links between school improvement initiatives and professional development strategies as driving forces for professional change are further investigated through collaborative projects across several continents. Within the limits of our remit, we have endeavoured to introduce an international dimension to our focus so that some degree of comparison and consideration can be given to the nature of developments across a broader spectrum. This is clearly a potentially fruitful area of work, with much scope for more work to be done.

We recognize that introducing such breadth of scope may exacerbate existing tensions between the concept of 'training on the job' and 'developing the whole professional': bringing to the fore potentially controversial issues concerning the relationship between increasing skill levels and a training 'competency' focus, thereby potentially diminishing the level of teacher 'professionalism'. Nevertheless, we consider that an international dimension offers valuable, if inevitably limited, opportunities for comparing policy and practice. Hopefully, it will also provoke valuable opportunities for reflection.

We also recognize that both the local environment and specific cultural backdrop within an organization has a significant impact within any review of developments. Differences in on-the-ground practices are vital and essential spurs to further development if the diverse needs of individual staff, groups, or even whole institutions, are to be met, since each one may be at very different 'starting' or 'growth' points on their own development continuum. Our aims in writing this book were, and remain, relatively modest. We readily acknowledge the complexity of professional development issues and relationships, and accept that no simple or single formula is capable of meeting the multiplicity of challenges facing those responsible for managing and participating in professional development.

We hope, nevertheless, that by setting out our research and by including practical suggestions for identifying and enhancing coherence in school-based CPD within the context of national and international developments, we may be able to contribute to the quickening debate concerning school improvement issues, led by effective educators and supported by continuing professional development.

CHAPTER 1

Establishing the Framework for Professional Development

Education Policy: A Focus on Change

This chapter outlines the framework of national and international policy development in education which has influenced CPD over recent decades. It begins by offering a brief overview of the social, political and economic influences which have underpinned educational developments during the post-war period. It also reviews the changing relationships between government, schools, LEAs and higher education institutions (HEIs) which have influenced the nature and management of INSET over recent years and goes on to consider the role played by CPD in developing strategies to promote 'school improvement' and 'school effectiveness'. The chapter concludes by briefly examining ways in which recent developments in England and Wales match professional development trends within the wider international context – in Europe, North America and Oceania.

While professional development is often regarded as an individual matter for teachers, there is growing recognition of its crucial role as an enabling mechanism at departmental and institutional levels for creating a professional culture in which improvement strategies can flourish. During the post-war period inservice education has experienced dramatic changes. We have moved from an expansion in HEI-centred provision, supported by government-funded teacher secondments, through the development of LEA-managed INSET with a substantial cadre of advisers, to the growth of an embryonic INSET marketplace, involving a range of providers and schools as 'customers' and 'clients' and an increase in personally funded development.

For many educationalists in Britain, change now appears to be endemic. In a series of legislative forays since the early 1980s, successive Conservative governments have established a range of initiatives in schools, further and higher education and, in doing so, have articulated the need for teachers to manage change rather than merely cope with the process. While this chapter (and indeed the book) focuses most specifically on the schooling system, many of the issues and strategies outlined here are congruent with those occurring in further and higher education. In order to assess the impact of change on the nature of teacher development over the past 15 years or so, we begin our review of the wider policy context by identifying three broad aspects of change.

First, change has been driven by government legislation – most importantly the 1988 Education Reform Act (ERA), which initiated an ongoing reframing of both the 'academic' and 'vocational' curriculum on a wide scale: in schools, further and higher education. Teachers have witnessed the introduction and review of the National Curriculum in schools (with hints of national curricula for higher and further education) and the introduction of National Vocational Qualifications (NVQs) accompanied by a focus on 'competency' at management levels through, for example, the Management Charter Initiative (MCI).

Second, we have seen changes to the organization and management of education, through the establishment of more 'autonomous' management in all sectors of education. We now have what Caldwell and Spinks (1988) have termed 'self-managing' schools as well as 'incorporated' or independent colleges and universities, where governing bodies have significantly greater responsibilities and control.

New funding patterns have been established across all sectors, giving greater local financial control – and a major focus on accountability. For example, the 1988 Education Reform Act initiated the demise of LEA financial control over schools, with budgets delegated for site-based management and the establishment of grant maintained schools (GMS). Within the tertiary sector, further education colleges gained independent status by 1992, with funding overseen by the Further Education Funding Council (FEFC). At the same time, the binary divide between LEA-maintained polytechnics and universities disappeared, with both kinds of institution being deemed universities funded through the Higher Education Funding Councils for England (HEFCE), Wales (HEFCW) and Scotland (SHEFC).

Third, during the 1990s, substantial and ongoing changes have been taking place in the structure and nature of teacher education, particularly in pre-service teacher education where we have seen a government-driven movement towards 'school-focused' – or even school-centred – initial teacher education. In addition, and less obviously perhaps, there have been changes in the management and control of inservice education, through tighter government funding mechanisms and the development of government-sponsored or targeted training.

The establishment of the Teacher Training Agency (TTA) in 1994, a quango with responsibility for both initial and inservice teacher education in England and Wales, has brought an even greater immediacy to an already rapidly changing scene. Clearly, within the limits of this chapter it is impossible to deal comprehensively with the array of changes which have influenced teachers' professional development over recent decades. Nevertheless, by placing broader CPD initiatives within their historical context, we are better able to track developments in INSET perceptions, policy and practice and establish a clearer framework for understanding how professional development is being managed within schools and colleges.

Transformations in Teacher Education: The Policy Context

For much of the post-war period, CPD and INSET in England and Wales remained very much the 'Cinderella' of teacher education (Williams, 1991), largely ignored by government in policy debates, frequently side-stepped in legislation, and too often the subject of 'recommendation and pragmatic action' (Burgess, 1993). Nevertheless, despite this apparent neglect, both the structures and relationships around teachers' professional development have undergone significant change over recent years, often because initiatives elsewhere in the education service have had a 'knock-on' effect on the nature of inservice provision.

We turn initially, therefore, to the policy framework surrounding teachers' professional development, In the immediate aftermath of the Second World War, education alongside welfare and employment became a high priority on the government's reconstruction agenda and education policy development was framed by cross-party consensus. The 1944 'Butler' Education Act was passed in the same year as the Beveridge Report with its focus on the welfare state and Keynes' *White Paper on Employment* which sought to establish 'high and stable employment'. Indeed, the thinking behind both the Beveridge and Keynes documents was influential in developing the pattern of post-war education provision. In line with the 1944 Education Act's commitment to 'education for all' at both primary and secondary levels as well as its commitment to raising the school-leaving age, policy-makers acknowledged the need to provide, with some rapidity, a trained teaching force capable of meeting the new demands.

The McNair Commission, set up to 'investigate the sources of supply and the methods of recruitment and training of teachers' (Board of Education, 1944), reported that there was a need to remedy the inadequacies of pre-service teacher training provision in order to meet the expanding demand for teachers. In addition, McNair made a plea for improved inservice provision, recommending that 'refresher and other courses' should be widely available and that 'necessary arrangements' should be made for 'teachers to be allowed sabbatical terms and in helping them to make the best use of them'. So while INSET was acknowledged as a valuable element in teacher education, for McNair it comprised little more than short, updating courses.

In your experience...

How far do you think that you and your colleagues think of professional development as comprising 'updating' or 'refresher' courses? Do you think policy-makers see it in this way today? Is this how INSET is used in most schools and colleges? If so, why might this be?

It may be that most of the INSET undertaken and funded by your own institution focuses on 'refreshing', 'updating' or 'awareness raising', since rapid changes and new initiatives expose our need for new knowledge. Over recent years, refresher courses and updating events have become commonplace, first because it is often easier to justify instrumentally focused *training* rather than more broadly based conceptions of *development;* second, it is cheaper than longer-term development-focused work; and third, because of imperatives to introduce massive 'instructional training' at speed in order to implement, for example, GCSEs, the National Curriculum and NVQs.

Between 1944 and 1950 there was a clear emphasis on the emergency training of new teachers with the immediate focus resting, not surprisingly, on initial training rather than inservice. The period up to 1970 also saw considerable expansion, both within the schools sector and in teacher education and training. As the schools system expanded, there were major implications for further and higher education, both of which needed to increase provision to meet rising student demand and to support this expansion with appropriately trained staff. However, the strategy of expansion harboured difficulties. For example, while the Robbins Report (DES, 1963) encouraged an expansion and consolidation of teacher education, only a decade later, in the mid-1970s, teacher training faced considerable contraction and rationalization as a result of reviewed demographic trends and a developing oil crisis and economic recession.

The 1970s were, in consequence, a period of transition which ended with the fracturing of the longstanding post-war liberal consensus around education policy which had involved the three key players responsible for the education service. This tripartite club – the Department of Education and Science, LEAs and teachers/teacher unions – had somewhat cosily overseen policy developments. Consensus had undoubtedly brought beneficial developments, such as the establishment of teachers' centres, which demonstrated LEA commitments to teacher development and acted as a precursor to school-based approaches to inservice education. However, the club was also a 'triangle of tension' (Briault, 1976), which bred conflict – particularly in connection with the contested concept of 'progressive education' and the 'failures' of comprehensivization. Ultimately, the 'triangle of tension' led to what Ball (1990) describes as a 'discourse of derision', with New Right elements in the Thatcher government openly deriding what they saw as rampant 'progressivism'. The 1972 James Report (DES, 1972a) had placed considerable emphasis on the importance of teachers' professional development, calling for reforms to initial training provision and arguing for a three-stage cycle of teacher education and training, comprising personal education; pre-service education and training; and inservice education and training. The major focus of the report was the importance of the third cycle, INSET:

> A large expansion of third cycle provision to give every teacher an
> entitlement to regular inservice education and training is an essential
> precondition of a more realistic and rational approach to initial training in the
> second cycle. (Para. 1.9, James Committee of Inquiry, DES, 1972)

Importantly, the concept of teacher entitlement was taken up again later in the report, when it was asserted that 'all teachers should be entitled to release with pay for a minimum of one school term or the equivalent (a period of say, 12 weeks) in a specified number of years' – an aim which remains unrealized over 30 years later. The government's White Paper, *Education: A Framework for Expansion* (DES, 1972b), introduced later the same year by Margaret Thatcher, the then Education Secretary in Edward Heath's Conservative government, echoed many of the James Report's proposed changes. However, the White Paper in effect represented the peak of the old 'expansionist' focus in government education policy. From 1973 on, the OPEC oil crisis and economic recession brought a sharp decline in public spending and, along with falling school rolls from the late 1970s, hastened the contraction in teacher education and training.

By the end of the 1970s, increasing tensions within the triangular partnership of DES, LEAs and teacher unions were progressively characterized by conflicts over teacher accountability, the degree of government control over the curriculum, and the level of education resourcing during economic recession. The marker for these fractured relationships was laid down in

Labour Prime Minister James Callaghan's 1976 Ruskin College speech, when he attacked what he claimed were a range of educational inadequacies in relation to the 'secret garden' of the school curriculum and school organization, and the inability of schools to prepare pupils for work. Arguably, he vocalized a growing disquiet – expressed most vociferously by New Right Conservatives through the Black Papers published between 1966 and 1977 – and attempted to steal the New Right's thunder by addressing the perceived failures of comprehensivization (CCCS, 1981). Callaghan's speech made public a debate which, in many respects, only reached a crescendo with the passage of the 1988 Education Reform Act. The 'Great Debate' which flowed from his comments heralded the first obvious tightening of central government control over the curriculum and assessment, with, for example, the issuing of Circular 14/77, which required LEAs to establish clearer and more formal curriculum policies. For a decade from 1979 onwards, successive Thatcher governments capitalized on a growing neo-Conservative disquiet articulating, in particular, the need to return to 'traditional values', 'standards' and 'choice' in a more responsive 'education marketplace'. This, the New Right asserted with growing confidence, would diminish what they perceived as the influence of the 'educational establishment' (eg, those working in education departments in higher education) and 'progressive' educationists in schools (eg, those apparently sympathetic to child-centred approaches).

Bolstered by right-wing think tanks like the Centre for Policy Studies, the Adam Smith Institute and the Institute of Economic Affairs (which, in the context of the 1980s, appeared to be prepared to 'think the unthinkable' in education policy terms), successive Thatcher governments sought to inject a market-forces and business-oriented approach into education. This, they argued, would facilitate increased consumer choice, efficiency and economy. A series of legislative interventions during the 1980s progressively undermined LEA control of education. However, the major piece of legislation – the 1988 Education Reform Act – was only introduced in the third Thatcher term, once the New Right's agenda for educational reform had gained momentum.

In establishing open enrolment, parental choice and local management of schools (LMS), which ensured that school funding was attached to pupil numbers, the 1988 Act created the embryonic 'education market' framework so beloved of the New Right. By the early 1990s the degree of centralization was clearly evident: the Secretary of State for Education gained considerable additional discretionary powers with the 1988 Act. This centralization was accompanied by a simultaneous (and in certain respects contradictory) delegation of day-to-day responsibility for the delivery of the curriculum, personnel management and budgetary responsibility to schools and colleges

13

themselves. LEAs were, in effect, being squeezed out of their key remit of control.

During the early 1990s, both Major governments have maintained the Thatcherite focus on market-driven philosophies in their approach to restructuring the schooling system. However, the government focus has been further broadened to incorporate another aspect of the educational jigsaw – the reform of teacher education, and in particular, initial teacher training (ITT). The government asserted that by allowing schools and colleges to be involved in (or even to control) ITT, the quality of output, ie, the quality of new teachers, would improve. In effect, it was argued, 'progressive' liberal ideas and the 'education establishment' agenda which were still being disseminated through the HEI monopoly of teacher training (what Kenneth Baker, the Secretary of State for Education, described as 'producer capture') would be broken, just as the LEAs' perceived stranglehold of the schooling system was also being broken. The apparently 'unthinkable' continued to be thought and acted upon.

In the schools sector, the 1992 Education Act effectively dismantled the long-standing inspection system in England and Wales, reliant on HMI by replacing it with a new body – OFSTED. In further education, the new FEFC established its own inspectorate along similar lines and the HEFCs and the Higher Education Quality Council (HEQC) also established inspection, audit and teaching assessment systems.

This series of policy developments in both schooling and teacher training systems provides the framework for assessing the 'on the ground' realities of INSET management and development. During the educational reforms of the 1980s and early 1990s, CPD remained very much in the half-shadows of the education debate, often influenced and implicated in various changes taking place in schools and initial training, but never centre-stage. In effect, CPD experienced change largely as a by-product of developments elsewhere in the system: For example, National Curriculum implementation, the introduction of local management and the establishment of appraisal in schools and colleges all led to significant demands for particular kinds of CPD and INSET, making it increasingly reactive in approach.

Alterations in funding patterns during this period also tended to destabilize providers' attempts to plan proactively for long-term development. The increasing government focus on annual and changing CPD priorities and funding strategies has pushed providers towards more short-termist, 'flavour of the month' approaches, discouraging more strategic staff planning, and making them reliant, instead, on part-time, contracted staff for 'quick response' programmes. We now consider in more detail the ways in which continuing professional development has been implicated in these changes.

Privatizing INSET: Towards a Professional Development Market

Despite the commitment to teachers' professional development which had been shown by the James Report, echoed by the government's Advisory Committee on the Supply and Training of Teachers (ACSTT; DES, 1978), and reaffirmed by the Advisory Committee on the Supply and Education of Teachers (ACSET; DES, 1984), professional development structures established in the post-war period did not change radically until the mid-1980s.

However, over the past decade or so the value of INSET has been increasingly formally recognized. The developing recognition was emphasized, for example, in *Better Schools* (DES, 1985), which argued that 'individual teachers need support and encouragement for their professional development at all stages of their career'. The School Teachers' Pay and Conditions of Employment proposals later in the decade (1987) also highlighted the importance of teacher development (with its focus on the introduction of teacher appraisal) and the specific identification of five 'professional development days' a year for those working in schools and colleges.

Furthermore, various training initiatives established during the 1980s encouraged a reframing of professional development. The government's experience with the introduction of TVEI (1983), alongside the lessons learned from 'cascading' GCSE training (1986) and the implications of the proposed National Curriculum, stimulated a review of both the costs and strategies in developing new provision and emphasized, in the government's mind, the importance of INSET which was directly relevant to classroom practice, rather than focused on general principles.

Although the various commitments to teacher development in the 1970s and 1980s were reflected in a gradual movement towards school-focused inservice education (Bolam, 1982b), significant structural change only began with the publication of Circular 6/86 (DES, 1986) which established the Local Education Authority Training Grants Scheme (LEATGS). It also marked an end to the relatively longstanding 'pool' of INSET funding which had enabled the more opportunist (and some argued far-sighted) LEAs to provide long-term development opportunities for their teachers. The 'pool' was, in effect an open-ended government funding commitment which some LEAs exploited to their teachers' advantage. The change to LEATGS represented a move towards more nationally prioritized, government-directed INSET funding, while still retaining a locally prioritized (ie, LEA-directed) element.

Consequently, the roles characterizing traditional INSET relationships between government, schools, LEAs and higher education altered as, initially, LEAs took a more central role in the planning and structuring of professional

15

development. However, the government's 'scrutiny' report on INSET in 1990, was followed by the introduction of GEST (Grant for Education Support and Training) in 1991, as a replacement for both LEATGS and ESGs (Education Support Grants) which were rolled up into one unitary grant, effectively ending the opportunity for 'local' (ie, LEA) funding priorities.

LEATGS funding arrangements had enabled LEAs to invest in more 'formalized and coherent' management systems (Harland *et al.*, 1993) and establish a cadre of key personnel – often advisory teachers – who brought a greater degree of professionalism into needs identification and delivery. Arguably, these developments made LEAs better prepared for the challenges of GEST. However, with GEST's introduction, traditional LEA support mechanisms declined as schools were progressively encouraged to adopt 'purchaser' and 'consumer' roles in the new INSET marketplace. The start of this move away from LEA-controlled professional development in which they were the virtual monopoly providers of non-award bearing INSET was outlined by Baker (1986) almost a decade ago and anticipated the development of a 'restructured INSET' (Harland *et al.*, 1993) which has brought a focus on privatization and the establishment of a 'professional development business' in education (Law and Glover, 1995).

Two things happened with the establishment of GEST: on one side, INSET funding became progressively more centralized and, on the other, accountabilities and responsibilities for its use were increasingly devolved to schools. By the mid-1990s, national rather than local priorities have taken precedence and increasing numbers of LEAs have dismantled their 'command and control cultures' in order to survive in the new climate. They have become (and in some cases are still becoming, with greater or lesser success) 'servicing' and 'facilitating' agencies (Morris, 1990).

The locus of INSET's day-to-day management now rests with schools and designated school staff. Professional Development Coordinators (PDCs) negotiate possible provision with their LEAs, who have become only one of a range of agencies bidding to 'get the business'. Despite 'ring fencing' between some LEAs (eg, whereby agreements are made not to 'poach' across old LEA boundaries), a greater competitive edge has developed. Alongside changes to national and local inspection structures following the 1992 Education (Schools) Act, this has tended to drive a wedge between some LEAs and their schools, especially since inspectors and advisers have become constrained by the need to undertake OFSTED inspection work in order to fund their own posts, which in turn inhibits their ability to maintain the flexibility of previous advisory and INSET relationships.

While changes brought by GEST created initial anxieties in schools, forcing many to decide whether to 'go it alone' or 'buy back' their LEA as a complete service-level package, schools also saw the potential benefits in having greater freedom of choice, even if it meant coping with restricted INSET budgets. Thus, traditional LEA-school relationships were threatened (and, in some cases, have disappeared) and many LEAs have, willingly or not, moved from 'management by control' to 'management by contract' (Harland *et al.*, 1993).

Increased competition between providers has established a realignment of old tripartite relationships traditionally linking schools with LEAs and higher education, while government set out the funding and stood to one side. In effect, recent developments have left schools as the ring-holders, now often the funding agents, organizers as well as consumers of inservice education and training. In some cases the more 'entrepreneurial' schools have taken an even more active part in the INSET marketplace, by becoming both consumers *and* training providers, sometimes involved in ITT partnerships with higher education as well as in their own INSET provision, which they market locally (or even nationally).

Influential arguments in favour of greater 'site-based' training and support have been articulated by, amongst others, the School Management Task Force (SMTF; DES, 1990) whose report reflected growing pressures to explore competence-based management training and assessment. Particular pressures for an examination of competence-based approaches also emanated from the Department of Employment and Department for Education and the Management Charter Initiative (Earley, 1992; Elliott, 1991a; Gealy, 1993; Whitty and Wilmott, 1991). Working collaboratively with regionally based LEA consortia to develop and promote school-based management training with a view to establishing greater flexibility of provision for school managers, the SMTF model promoted school-focused and school-based developments.

In your experience...

What advantages might schools and colleges gain by becoming involved as providers and development centres, whether in pre-service or inservice work? Are there any disadvantages, either for institutions or the individuals who work and learn in them?

As schools and colleges have taken on new professional responsibilities in initial teacher training 'partnerships' and for managing the professional development of their staff, you may consider it is an obvious next step for them to become providers, through offering their developing expertise (and possibly their venue) to others and operationalizing the concept of a 'learning organization' (NCE, 1993). Expertise in determining and meeting professional needs is increasingly to be found and valued in schools and colleges. However, some schools recognize that this new focus also brings the dangers of increased insularity, professional overload and a potential for 'recycling inadequacies'. These dangers now need to be faced along with the central question facing schools and colleges about whether such developments are compatible with their core mission and role – to educate pupils and students.

Each new initiative has stimulated the need for institutions to rethink the nature of teacher development policies and practices themselves. For example, realistically, how far can a school encourage its teachers to become teacher training mentors or INSET trainers without the institution having a clear professional development focus and policy itself? In many cases, these issues are only now beginning to be addressed.

The National Commission on Education has suggested that schools may evolve into American-style 'learning shops': institutional training and re-source bases which meet teachers' learning needs as well as those of pupils or students (NCE, 1993). By taking over the management of professional development funding, schools have also accepted a multitude of management responsibilities for planning, decision-making and resourcing teachers' professional support. It is this additional and sometimes overwhelming workload aspect which raises grave concerns within institutions themselves. We consider this issue further in Chapter 5.

In addition, the TTA has developed initiatives like HEADLAMP (Headteachers' Leadership, Administration and Management Programme) and the National Professional Qualification, identifying schools (or more precisely governing bodies) as CPD purchasing agents. The HEADLAMP scheme targets newly appointed heads, providing governing bodies with up to £2500 of support (for courses, consultancy, mentoring, work-shadowing, industrial placements, etc) following their appointment of a new headteacher. Support must be bought in from TTA-registered providers comprising LEAs, HEIs and a range of private providers who, importantly, must agree to possible inspection of their provision by OFSTED in order to become TTA registered. The planned National Professional Qualification (NPQ) targets aspiring headteachers (ie, middle managers and deputy heads) and continues the trend of locking providers more closely into the professional development market-place and encouraging a more competitive 'business' mindset.

As schools have established school-based and school-managed approaches to inservice work, higher education has had to adjust to the new scenario and has, in some ways, become marginalized (Day, 1989). Traditionally, universities and colleges offered teachers long-term development opportunities, with secondments for a term or a year onto award-bearing programmes (eg, Masters degrees and advanced Diplomas), with a ready-made research base and direct links into a professional community of scholars.

With the abandonment of the 'pool' funding system, universities and colleges saw a relatively rapid decline in registrations for long courses. GEST reinforced this trend through increased nationally targeted funding and a progressive year-on-year erosion of local, LEA-set priority funding. Funding changes and teacher-as-consumer pressures have meant that higher education is moving away from traditional 'provider-recipient' relationships with schools towards, on the one hand, professional training partnerships, eg, for shared initial training, and, on the other, towards 'customer-marketeer' relationships, where schools negotiate what they want to purchase in the marketplace. Universities can no longer count on being traditional 'expert-providers' and, instead, are progressively modifying themselves into what Gilroy and Day (1993) have called 'learning support agencies'.

In essence, then, higher education is nowadays confronted by the twin pressures of consumerism and quality assessment, which has driven a review of its activity and provision. Like LEAs, universities and colleges offering CPD opportunities need to satisfy 'consumer demand' within a constrained 1990s economic climate, where government-determined funding priorities have become central. In addition, they need to meet the 'quality' imperative: ensuring that courses are delivered, monitored and evaluated with a focus on high quality provision, regardless of the difficulties of establishing precisely what the concept of 'quality' means (Pfeffer and Coote, 1991).

In your experience...

What kind of professional relationship does your own school or college have with its local education authority and higher education institutions? In what ways have these relationships changed in recent years? Has your job become easier or more difficult in consequence?

This may be a difficult issue for you to consider since there is now a real diversity of relationships between schools and colleges and providing 'agencies' like LEAs and HEIs. The opening up of a new INSET 'market' has meant that both LEAs and higher education institutions (HEIs) have, to a lesser or greater degree, begun to develop a service focus reflecting their new 'client-provider' relationships with schools and colleges. Professional relationships are therefore in a process of transition: your LEA may be the main 'servicing agent' or only one of many providers. While many of the traditional relationships which schools had established with LEAs and HEIs may have survived INSET privatization, they are now characterized by fewer long-term certainties and a greater precariousness of provision, which may, in turn, create difficulties for teachers wishing to plan for the future.

The introduction of GEST and new OFSTED inspection structures forced LEAs to review their operations to become 'leaner and fitter' organizations able to survive the new competition. The early retirement of experienced advisers and inspectors, coinciding with the introduction of a government-encouraged marketized education system, has led to a relatively rapid if uneven explosion in private consultancies working with schools and colleges.

Private providers have supplemented their ranks by using early retirees from HMI and higher education – so-called 'grey power' – as consultants. Nevertheless, while there is often great expertise in the ranks of private consultancies, as schools have become increasingly preoccupied with 'value for money' issues the level of competition has increased and quality has become a central concern. Although the initial growth in private provision also brought its fair share of 'cowboy providers' and 'quick fixers', with glossy brochures and 'not to be missed' offers showered on schools and colleges, institutions show increasing reluctance to engage relatively unknown providers with untraceable pedigrees.

These issues raise important questions for those involved in professional development, whether as provider or 'client'. How far has INSET privatization and an educational market benefited pupils in schools, their teachers and the INSET community itself? Undoubtedly, the presence of highly professional and tightly organized private consultancies has exposed some of the earlier inability of LEAs and higher education to maintain 'closeness to the customer' (Peters and Waterman, 1982) and to compete in a more openly competitive scene. Viewed from a school's perspective, private consultancies may have helped to sharpen the financial edge of buying-in INSET and have kept more traditional (ie, LEA and HEI) providers on their toes. However, while their presence has encouraged a movement away from a straightforward 'course focus' towards the school-based 'consultancy focus', schools nevertheless also report that too often their quality remains highly variable and risky.

In examining the nature of professional support available to schools over recent years, it is important to recognize the potential (though still contested) role of OFSTED in stimulating schools to achieve higher standards of teaching and learning through regular inspection. Part of the importance here is that there is an openly accessed Framework for Inspection and much recent CPD has been centred on disseminating the criteria for successfully 'passing' inspection. With its motto, 'improvement through inspection', OFSTED appears to see itself as complementary to professional development and inservice education, though this view is challenged by many who see inspection as potentially undermining of self-review and development. The next section takes up some of the issues surrounding inspection and professional development.

Inspection, Improvement and Professional Development

Although many teachers regard professional development as personally highly beneficial (HMI, 1993) it is also potentially a powerful tool for achieving wider organizational and professional goals. It is this last aspect which has been increasingly stressed by the British government in the context of teacher education funding.

During the last decade and a half, legislation and government initiatives have brought an increasingly strong focus on the education market and quality issues. Arguably, once a more prescriptive National Curriculum was introduced alongside financial delegation and personnel management, it was inevitable that the government would begin to identify more rigorous methods of monitoring and evaluating institutional and teacher performance, whether in schools, colleges or further and higher education. Inspection as a way of auditing achievement and checking improvement is now high on the government's agenda.

This increased focus on institutional performance, teaching quality and school improvement and school effectiveness issues means that professional development is a potentially important strategy for achieving higher standards. Although over recent years schools have been centre-stage in the 'standards' debate, similar trends are identifiable elsewhere in education, with both further and higher education establishing their own performance indicators, 'quality' agendas and institutional audits.

While HMI had traditionally inspected without disclosing to schools the details of its key criteria – plant, match, pedagogy, progression, professionalism and climate (Pearce, 1986) – OFSTED has opened the process to greater public and professional scrutiny, articulating the criteria on which judgements are made. In doing so it has provoked debate and provided what has seemed an overwhelming level of detail on both the system and criteria used. While the old HMI system meant that schools were likely to be inspected only infrequently – perhaps not even in a professional lifetime – OFSTED currently targets schools for inspection every four years, with the effectiveness and efficiency of teaching, learning and support being central elements in their scrutiny. However, it remains a matter of major debate how far improvement and development can be 'inspected into' schools.

Schools have shown growing concern about the impact of inspection and the ways in which it may skew the focus of professional development within institutions. The new inspection process focuses on providing schools, government, parents and public with a picture of school and teacher effectiveness. As a consequence, a major educational industry is being built around 'school improvement and effectiveness', providing schools with details of school improvement strategies and the key features of school effectiveness. For example, the NCE, an independent enquiry into long-term education development in the UK, established in 1991, has identified a range of success indicators, which if adapted slightly, may be appropriate for other educational institutions (see Box 1.1).

Box 1.1: Key features of successful educational institutions

1. Strong, positive leadership by senior managers, particularly the principal.
2. A good atmosphere or ethos, developed out of shared aims and values and efforts to create a stimulating and attractive physical environment.
3. High and consistent expectations of all students.
4. A clear and continuing focus on teaching and learning.
5. Well-developed procedures for assessing how students are progressing.
6. Responsibility for learning shared by the students themselves.
7. Participation by students in the life of the institution.
8. Rewards and incentives which encourage students to succeed.
9. Wider parental and community involvement in students' education and in supporting the aims of the institution.

(Adapted from National Commission on Education, 1993)

In theory, as institutional improvement strategies become better utilized and, as teachers' roles and responsibilities are acknowledged as highly complex and dependent on a vast array of skills, knowledge and abilities, the use of narrower definitions of staff or professional development (eg, the 'quick fix', one-day event and refresher course) will become progressively more redundant.

While the concept of professional development must undoubtedly encompass opportunities to develop more effective teaching skills, strategies and styles, it also needs to incorporate opportunities for teacher development within a whole-school cultural development, where, for example, teachers know and practice ways of enhancing and supporting student learning. Teachers also need to establish more proactive professional relationships as part of a learning culture (where staff also see themselves as learners) and evaluate and monitor not just their students' development, but their own as well. In addition, they need to initiate and implement new ideas and strategies, whether at a classroom or institutional level.

Joyce (1991) identifies five 'doors' to institutional improvement which, he suggests, may open 'a passageway into the culture of the school' and demonstrate how professional development, as part of a broader, more integrated strategy, can help to underpin institutional improvement (see Box 1.2).

Box 1.2: Five 'doors' to institutional improvement

1. *Collegiality:* creating a culture through developing cohesive and professional relationships between staff (and the wider community), in which 'broad vision-directed improvements as well as day-to-day operations' are valued.
2. *Research:* familiarizing staff with research findings into school improvement, teaching effectiveness etc. which can support 'in-house' development.
3. *Site-specific information:* enabling and encouraging staff to collect and analyse data on students, schools and effects of change – both as part of a formal evaluation and informally.
4. *Curriculum initiatives:* collaborating with others to introduce change in their own subject area and on a cross-curricular basis.
5. *Instructional initiatives:* enabling staff to develop their teaching skills and strategies, through eg generic teaching skills, repertoires of teaching methods, specific teaching styles or approaches.

(Joyce, 1991)

Using Joyce's 'doors', professional development is likely to become more 'integrated with' rather than 'bolted onto' other aspects of school development. Individual and departmental needs may be identified as part of whole-school, curricular and cross-curricular development, rather than being reactive afterthoughts which only allow people to 'cope' with and not 'manage' change. This clearer focus on integrated development complements trends towards utilizing, as appropriate, more rational planning procedures in schools and colleges. These, in turn, have been stimulated, first through the formal requirement on schools to produce school development plans (SDP); second, through OFSTED's and FEFC's inspection processes which require institutions to develop action plans; and third, through the introduction of school-based management processes, eg, budgetary responsibilities and statutory National Curriculum requirements.

While most schools and colleges have only limited experience of establishing integrated rational planning processes at individual, departmental or whole-school planning levels, increasing numbers are making genuine progress with development planning, often facilitated by a growing awareness of the potential benefits gained through institutional self-evaluation. This, in turn, is being facilitated by teachers' broader perceptions of their roles stemming from 'teacher as researcher' opportunities often linked to further professional qualifications, which enable them to scrutinize and evaluate more formally their own classroom practice.

OFSTED has pointed to the centrality of leadership and the headteacher/ principal role. While headship has predominantly been equated with the concept of the 'leading professional' (Hughes, 1972), recent emphases on market and industrial models of management may endanger this, particularly where institutional leaders are required to demonstrate appropriate business, personnel and accountancy skills above their curriculum development and teaching skills. At one extreme, governing body appointment committees may no longer consider headteachers and principals as *primus inter pares* (first amongst equals) but emphasize instead the importance of the 'chief executive' role.

While the focus on site-based management tended, at least initially, to emphasize this trend it is, in fairness, not entirely new. For example, almost two decades ago, *Ten Good Schools* (HMI, 1977) emphasized the substantial professional learning needs of heads, especially because they have ultimate responsibility for institutional quality and the development needs of colleagues. In addition, Hall *et al.*'s study *Headteachers at Work* (1986) pointed out that many heads fail to undertake effectively enough a range of professional tasks, particularly those linked to professional development.

More recently, the issue has risen near the top of the TTA's agenda. In addition to overseeing a substantial review of teacher pre-service and inservice training, its methodology and funding, it has a developing profile as an initiator of new developments. Consequently, despite the TTA's stress on the need for more strategically planned professional development, its work retains a strong 'immediacy' focus. It remains an interesting question whether the concept of a headteacher as a 'leading professional' and the 'chief executive' can be integrated effectively using these TTA strategies. We now turn to consider the wider international context within which professional development takes place and to consider how far experience in England and Wales compares with that elsewhere in the world.

The International Context for Professional Development

Over the past decade or so, relatively longstanding assumptions about the broad context of education and the specifics of teacher education have been undergoing review in several parts of the world. For example, in much of Europe, North America and Australia we have witnessed a developing critique – particularly though not exclusively amongst Conservative and right-wing governments – of educational standards and teacher quality. These concerns have been expressed in relation to student achievement and how far the system and teachers meet individual student needs, reflecting a view that there are too many 'flung aside, forgotten children' (Gow and McPherson, 1980). They have also been expressed in relation to the ability of various national education systems to 'deliver' results which match economic imperatives (Leclercq, 1988). In a review of the rationale for educational reform in the developed world, Levin (1994) posits 'the notion of not enough return for the resources invested in education', revealing the assumptions underpinning an economic perspective.

Economic decline and unemployment and the growth of New Right ideas in several countries has provoked increasing political concern over education quality in a fast-changing technological world. The notion of an information superhighway promises an increasingly internationalized education focus, with globalized communications and a vast potential expansion in access to 'know-how'. Singapore, for example, has led the Pacific rim countries in making information technology a key element and high priority in teacher skills development. Education is, more than ever, increasingly viewed by governments as central to economic success in a highly competitive, international environment. These concerns have been reflected in the development of more diversified schooling systems, which are apparently more able to cope with heterogeneous student populations and stress differentiated teaching and learning opportunities provided by a highly skilled, up-to-date teacher workforce.

Governments of various political persuasions across several continents have demanded closer scrutiny of the management of education, the nature of teacher training and the impact of professional development on classroom success. Led by the USA during the 1960s, a number of Western countries pursued educational reform by establishing, for example, more broadly based compulsory education systems, expanded post-compulsory provision, a higher school leaving age and a focus on equality of opportunity (Elliott and MacLennan, 1994).

However, by the early 1980s these orthodoxies were being openly challenged in Europe as well as North America and Australia. With Britain leading the way, a number of countries have revised their educational priorities, particularly as industrial decline, technological change and economic constraints have forced the pace of change (Neave, 1992). This increasing emphasis on the importance of education to economic development and prosperity has provoked a revaluing of teachers' inservice provision. As Pepin (1995) notes, this has led to a revised concept of the role of INSET, bringing a stronger emphasis on 'lifelong learning' and 'continuing' development, as well as a recognition that INSET 'serves as a catalyst for the continuous adjustments which have to be made in dynamic systems' (p.8).

Conservative policy-makers in the USA and Canada have also concentrated on issues of accountability; on the notion of traditional morality and the maintenance of 'high standards'; and on the apparent need to instil 'business' values, the concept of 'choice' and an acceptance of the 'market' into education. In essence, these countries have followed a similar though in some respects a less sharply defined agenda, to that adopted by Thatcher and Major governments in England and Wales during the 1980s and 1990s (Elliott and MacLennan, 1994).

Within the Australian context, the late 1980s and early 1990s also saw a developing discontinuity between the liberal-progressive reforms of the 1970s and increasing government attempts to link education more closely with business and vocational needs. A key Australian government aim has appeared to be the development of an 'education industry' (Knight, 1992), making Australia a 'clever country' with a multi-skilled, flexible workforce (Knight, *et al.*, 1991). In addition, Australian government publications like *Teachers Learning: Improving Australian schools through inservice teacher training and development* (DEET, 1988) articulate its attempts to reconstruct teacher education as a support for its economic imperatives and changed circumstances.

Pepin (1995), in a review of inservice provision within the European Union and EFTA/EEA countries, stresses the development of a growing European consensus over the objectives of inservice training. This incorporates, first the need to meet teacher's personal and professional development; second, the need to improve the quality of education through a focus on teaching, the curriculum and school organization; and third, the need to enhance teachers' knowledge and understanding of 'the social and environmental milieu'. While not all countries clearly articulate this third objective, Pepin asserts that there is a remarkable degree of commonality in focus overall.

For example, several European governments have acknowledged that initial teacher training is only a preparatory period and not sufficient development for a career-long professional role (Blackburn and Moisan, 1987). Rather than being a simple 'cure-all' for the deficiencies of ITT, inservice education is increasingly regarded as a complex and lifelong process, with countries like

Germany, Norway and Iceland formally identifying two inservice strands: 'continuing' training (upgrading and updating professional skills and knowledge) and 'additional' or 'qualifying' training (which allows for certificated learning).

While CPD is generally government-led within Europe, there is a growing trend towards decentralization, though the degree, level and implications vary considerably. While in countries like Belgium and Italy decentralization has been complicated by the national political framework, eg, federal structures and autonomous regions, there have been several attempts across Europe to develop common parameters and coordinating structures for INSET, though these largely focus on skills development.

Despite moves to place initial training within universities in most European countries (Archer and Peck, 1991), professional development is still largely located within non-university institutions, which sometimes creates accreditation difficulties. This issue is, however, much less of a problem within the British context, where schools, LEAs and professional associations have worked collaboratively with HEIs to develop a common accreditation framework.

INSET is generally an 'out of hours' activity in most European countries, although in some there are compulsory training sessions lasting between one day (eg, Belgium, France) and several days (eg, Ireland, Portugal, Finland, Sweden, Scotland, Norway). Elsewhere, INSET may be provided only 'when needed' (eg, Luxembourg, Austria), although in all countries some level of professional development is available on a voluntary basis.

INSET participation is generally accepted as a teachers' professional right, and its provision as the state's moral obligation, although there is little state compulsion for teachers to undertake CPD in most European countries. However, in Greece, newly appointed teachers undergo obligatory training, mainly because as much as ten years may elapse between teacher training and gaining an initial permanent teaching post. In addition, primary teachers in Luxembourg, Portugal and Spain are unable to advance their careers unless they undertake professional development.

Not surprisingly, perhaps, the major obstacle to INSET participation in most countries remains financial. Pepin (1995) notes the contradiction which arises where,

> teachers have a right to pursue professional development and a duty to
> update their knowledge, but these rights and duties are rarely considered
> obligatory, on the one hand because budgets do not allow for it, and on the
> other because training can have a positive effect only if it is desired and freely
> chosen. (p.22)

Little clarity exists regarding the national budgetary allocations for in-service education and training in European countries because the degree of variety is so great. There is, for example, no international agreement about which activities and personnel count, which sectors are included, which training funds derive from which government sources and so on. Overall, however, funding for INSET within Europe rarely amounts to more than 1 per cent of a country's total education budget (Pepin, 1995).

Classroom replacement or 'cover' for teachers undertaking INSET remains a block to participation across all countries, with each providing its own coping strategies depending on the nature of curriculum demands being faced. In England and Wales, the management of replacement and supply cover, once the responsibility of LEAs, has now fallen to individual schools. Teacher replacement occurs more frequently in primary than secondary education and tends to be approached on an individualized basis rather than through a legislative framework in most European countries. Even in France, Spain and Scotland, where a pool of replacement teachers is provided, the unpredictability of demand means that few rules are often in place.

Strategies used in many European countries to alleviate 'cover' problems include lesson exchanges between teachers; authorized non-replacement; 'out-of-hours' training offered by universities through summer schools and distance-learning; correspondence courses (especially for initial training or 'qualifying' courses); specific days/dates sets aside for specific curriculum areas (akin to the English and Welsh 'closure' days, originally known as 'Baker Days' after the Secretary of State, Kenneth Baker, who introduced them).

Because formalized INSET is a relatively recent phenomenon in a number of European states, only limited data exists concerning the degree of teacher participation. Too often incomplete statistics are kept, no longstanding database exists and varying degrees of decentralized responsibility creates coordination difficulties. Available evidence suggests that participation rates are low overall, though they are perhaps understandably higher when linked as a compulsory element with promotion and career advancement, as in Portugal and Spain. Participation rates in Denmark and the Netherlands are relatively high (with approximately one-third of teachers participating in some form of INSET each year) though very little is known about the nature and quality of INSET being offered, thus making it difficult to relate the nature of the demand with the actual supply available.

The picture of professional development internationally and particularly in Europe remains diverse and complex, inhibiting the possibility of overarching conclusions. Pepin (1995) argues that a clearer picture is only achievable through in-depth case studies deriving from several countries, particularly because international statistical data regarding INSET should be treated with caution. While comparative analysis remains elusive, the key issues are nevertheless common to many industrialized countries. There are similarities, for example, in terms of budgetary difficulties; the nature of INSET management and organization; the challenges involved in maximizing participation; the issues regarding voluntarism and compulsion; and the nature and timing of INSET. In addition, there is common concern with how far the focus should fall on state-funded or individually funded development, the links between development and career advancement, and the role of monitoring and evaluation.

A decade ago, when Blackburn and Moisan (1987) suggested that INSET 'is an essential area with an unstable structure' they identified the key problem confronting policy-makers. Without securing a national framework for professional development, individuals and their institutions are unable to fully exploit their potential.

CHAPTER 2

The Changing Scene

The Essence of Professional Development

The introduction to this book outlined briefly the structure and parameters of the Keele Effective Educators Project (KEEP), while the previous chapter considered the policy framework within which CPD has operated over the past decade and beyond. We now turn to INSET at a micropolitical level by outlining the ways in which the schools participating in the KEEP project identify the parameters of CPD and determine their strategies for pursuing their development remit. We begin by identifying more closely the ways in which professional development is conceived and operationalized by staff in the project schools.

There are differing views of the nature of professional development. In one case study secondary school, staff spoke of CPD solely as the 'training days' specified as part of their conditions of pay and service in the settlement of 1987; in another it was 'anything we do which does something to make us more efficient and effective'; and in one primary school it was seen as 'everything that we do together... and with only four staff it's difficult to know what is and what isn't professional development in some way'.

Like researchers, teachers tend to use the terms 'CPD', 'INSET', 'staff development' and 'teacher development' loosely and interchangeably, often interpreting them differently according to tradition, circumstance and context. When teachers and managers involved in our research were asked to offer their own personal definitions of INSET and CPD, there was, perhaps unsurprisingly, a relatively wide variation in individual emphasis. However, for many interviewees, meanings tended to cluster around the notion that CPD was more broadly conceived, centred on longer-term commitments, and was especially concerned with personal aspects of professionalism. Definitions of INSET tended to be more narrowly conceived, focused on institutional concerns and centred on short-term obligations to 'train' and 'update'.

Nevertheless, in general interviewees were clear that both conceptions contributed to improving their own professional practice and that of others, whether as classroom teachers or as managers.

In a description of professional development, Darling-Hammond *et al.* (1986) suggest that there are two types of development: that which grows from working alongside other professionals and promotes professional understanding; and that which promotes training to satisfy more objective measures like student success rates and is based on skills acquisition and developing competence. INSET experiences over the last decade have meant that a significant number of staff interviewees involved in KEEP were inclined to see CPD and INSET as immediacy-focused 'training' and were concerned with increasing their ability to cope with the requirements of a changing curriculum. They see this as a particular and necessary response to external pressures, such as more frequent inspection and external testing for National Curriculum key stages. Oldroyd and Hall (1991) argue that funding changes and government reforms have effectively 'shifted the provision of INSET towards professional training and away from professional education'. Many KEEP interviewees, however, appear to conceive that professional training may not be sufficient to deliver effective institutional improvements and there may be a need for more reflective development approaches.

The TTA's definition of CPD as the 'development of teachers' professional knowledge, understanding and skills so as to improve the quality of teaching and learning in the classroom' in their 1995 survey (Page and Fisher-Jones, 1995) is relatively broadly based, although the focus embodied in some of its initiatives appears to confirm an emphasis on training strategies within a developing competence framework, largely perhaps because its work is linked to the implementation of government reforms.

In your experience...

How do you and your colleagues define 'continuing professional development'? Do they focus on training for specific skills or do they use a broader concept of development? What might their views show about common values in the department, school or college where you work and what implications might their views have for future policy developments in your institution?

Your colleagues may identify a wide range of perceptions about CPD, though several may see it as strongly focused on 'training for yet another new initiative', as one teacher described it. Our research evidence suggests that approaches to CPD vary from the exclusive end of the spectrum, where the focus is often on single training activities, separately organized, managed and evaluated, to the inclusive end, where the range of opportunities for individuals are integrated and combined within an overall personal development plan and which now, in approaching 95 per cent of schools, relate to some degree with the institutional development plan (IDP).

The more exclusive focus is typified by the comment that, we offer a programme of training on the three training days related to what staff say that want through the annual GRIDS [Guidelines for the Review and Internal Development of Schools] process... if staff want individual courses we say yes as often as we can until there is no more money. The inclusive view, offered by one headteacher, is that:

> professional development is part of our philosophy of school improvement. We are trying to use every opportunity for development – be it through formal training sessions or informally through providing time for staff to watch each other at work... but everything is set against our criteria which relates to our need to enhance teaching and learning quality in line with the school development plan.

Our research shows that, for most schools, professional development is a combination of meeting three kinds of need:

- *individual need* – developing the skills and knowledge to teach effectively and to grow as a professional;
- *departmental, year or group need* – developing common approaches and sharing expertise within a team situation; and,
- *whole-institutional needs* – establishing common values which determine policies for the school.

The recent tendency to increased institutional autonomy has, however, limited an important fourth dimension:

- *multi-institutional needs* – where groups of schools worked cooperatively to establish area-wide values, and was exemplified, for example, by the 'effective schools' initiatives within Oxfordshire between 1986 and 1988 and the 'Network: Upper Secondary Education' in the Netherlands (Veuglers and Zijlstra, 1995) established in 1988, where schools 'use each others' professionalism'.

This last dimension often characterized particular LEA support strategies in the past, when they 'held the development ring'. Where more centralized systems continue to operate, as in British Columbia school districts, universities and school boards work together to offer a programme of curriculum development work at summer schools (Wideen and Holborn, 1990). This approach is backed up by continuing action research, enabling networks to be developed across groups of schools.

Activities and Strategies for Professional Development

In a review of changing strategies for teacher education, Kirk (1988) highlights the problems which arise from top-down initiatives, imposed on teachers to ensure they can more readily cope with imposed changes; and bottom-up initiatives, which grow and develop out of responses to staff-identified needs within the working environment.

Traditionally, inservice education was most frequently offered as long courses, secondments or short external courses, attended by one or more staff and then, depending on the focus, disseminated using a cascade model to others in the institution or local authority who might be interested. Long-course attendance usually led to a professional award, while shorter courses were rarely accredited. Although long-course and secondment sponsorship has declined dramatically over the past decade, much of the short-course focus and structure still persists in a number of LEAs. However, there has also been a rapidly growing recognition of the need for greater CPD flexibility to meet current and evolving needs. Change has been imposed for a number of reasons:

- because institutions as well as individuals need to achieve better value for money – a concern deriving from the presence of a declining funding base;
- through a pedagogic preference for action research;
- because teachers' professional work is increasingly framed by government concerns to establish 'education market' philosophies; and
- through the use of managed change models to encourage people to work cooperatively and to reflect both individually and collectively on their findings.

The rapidly changing pattern of professional development has been given added force by the impact of Schon's work (1983) which stresses the value of reflective opportunities, as well as Fullan's (1991) which links effective change with a sense of collective ownership by participants.

The multiplicity of activities linked to professional development in schools associated with the KEEP project suggests there is a growing awareness of the potential for both personal and group reflection on day-to-day professional practice which is leading to improved planning and evaluation. These activities appear to follow a sequence, which moves from the externally offered and operated, to the internally managed and controlled. This move can be seen, at the extremes, as a shift away from dispersed and provider-centred INSET where participants can too easily become relatively passive trainees there to have their content knowledge updated, towards more localized and school-centred development, where teachers in departments and classrooms are the active locus of attention, and the process as well as content of in-house change is crucial.

The balance between these two extremes has altered relatively rapidly over recent years. However, it is important to note that school-based and school-centred activities may sometimes be inappropriate or even counterproductive. If professional development is to succeed, then appropriate, coherent and timely strategies are essential. We now review some of the development opportunities available to schools.

Short Courses

These are offered as an off-site activity by external providers like LEAs or HEIs, and increasingly, by private providers. They 'offer quality at their best, but they're away from the school environment and cause more disruption than other activities... we need to know whether they'll be worthwhile'. This traditional INSET provision has advantages, where the purpose is to pass on information or to practise particular pedagogic or assessment processes, but there was some feeling amongst a cross section of staff in project schools that,

> except on the rare occasions where you hear a really charismatic speaker
> throwing out new ideas that really get you thinking about how you do things
> back at work, the impact of short courses is generally rather limited...
> generally, I'd have to say that it all evaporates after, well really... a few hours.

Conferences

These are again off-site, but involve 'bringing people together with like interests and with a clear idea of what they want to achieve'. This kind of development activity appears more acceptable to senior management teams in secondary schools as well as to primary heads (possibly for status reasons and the fact that such events are seen by participants as opportunities for profes-sional interchange rather than as 'training'). Examination board events and conferences are commended by the schools we researched for the way they facilitated subject-focused networks and the way moderation teams function.

Long Courses

These were particularly attractive to schools during the early 1980s when more generous funding was available for award-bearing INSET and many LEAs managed declining school rolls by encouraging a considerable degree of retraining through secondments. The advantages accrued during those years are now clearly evident in responses from senior staff in schools who were given management development opportunities at that time. A typical comment is that, 'it was the most significant single influence on my approach to school management and gave me the confidence to go on in my career'. The scheme collapsed when funding pressures grew.

Since 1988, most long-course development has been undertaken by individuals on a part-time, largely self-funded basis; although it is partially supported by school funding in 32 per cent of our responding schools in 1995, this was often on a token rather than substantial basis. While the main advantages clearly rest with the individual, there is a growing acceptance that 'our school gains from the new ideas and the contacts which are being built up'.

Each of these activities are external to the school and available on an offer basis. Since the changes to teachers' conditions of service in 1987 and the passage of the 1988 Education Reform Act, which altered management and funding structures, there has been an increase in internal activities in which all staff participate.

Professional Development Days/Training Days

Five designated days a year are set aside by the government when staff are free of teaching commitment and able to undertake further professional development and training. There has been growing concern expressed by the Department for Education and Employment, OFSTED, the TTA and researchers that these days have not always been used productively. Kerry (1993) suggests that weaknesses in planning, funding, organization and evaluation of such days inhibit their overall effectiveness.

Our own case study evidence shows that some professional development days are 'inappropriate because they are imposed rather than something which is based on staff needs'. Busher (1990), examining the way that one LEA organized its CPD work, suggests that success is related to how far

- participants feel a sense of ownership of the topic;
- the professional development environment is conducive to reducing the stresses of normal school life; and
- a shared value system is established where such activities are considered effective and important.

'Baker Days' were initially problematic because teachers frequently saw them as an expression of government power. In order to overcome such perceptions, costly attempts were sometimes made to emulate the environment of industrial conference provision, although as funding levels have fallen, there has been a more realistic use of cheaper alternatives.

According to many heads, staff are 'now accepting that these days provide a good opportunity to think about the issues in a school which affect us all'. Many teachers, however, still retain a sense of imposition and would 'prefer the opportunity to be able to get on with some of the planning and review work which would be of greatest benefit to the class I spend my time with'. One head acknowledges the instrumentalist tendency in the use of such days, since 'the impending inspection did much to concentrate the minds of the whole staff and each full day was seen as a chance to put our house in order'.

Group Activities

In order to overcome some of the disadvantages of traditionally organized INSET days, some schools have adopted more flexible arrangements which, although stretching administrative regulations to the hilt, allow groups to undertake development activities during twilight or weekend sessions. These groups tend to take a thematic approach, focusing on issues best facilitated by smaller planning and working units, which then feed their findings into whole-school or sometimes senior staff meetings.

Increased group or working party activities have been accompanied by a considerable proliferation of materials and packages adaptable for individual institutions. While some of these are available 'off the shelf', groups are also sometimes supported by external consultants who facilitate their use, although increasingly 'this is on our terms, to help us to do the work in our own situation'. More recently, these activities have been further enhanced through accrediting activities towards individual 'credit bank accounts' for professional awards.

Critical Friendship

The need for a catalyst for groups involved in managing change has also been recognized in some schools which buy-in the expertise of a critical friend for group or individual support. This role has been investigated by Bayne-Jardine and Holly (1994) who emphasize the importance of relationships based on mutual trust and growing confidence, so that comments and evaluations are valued by group members rather than viewed as criticisms.

Critical friendship strategies were used to support the Technical and Vocational Education Initiative (TVEI), which depended on work groups both within and between schools or colleges in an area, with staff bringing about change by 'holding a mirror to activities'. This form of consultancy has also been used to support a range of activities across different phases, eg, materials development for teaching industry-based topics within primary school clusters (where the critical friend was the director of a small business) and for developing a strategy to establish a business languages curriculum across a group of secondary schools (where the critical friend was a curriculum development specialist from a local university).

Distance Learning Developments

With or without a critical friend, the increasing availability of structured learning materials to support knowledge, skills and attitudes development has brought greater flexibility of learning opportunities. Modular degree schemes offering individual and, potentially, group accreditation contribute added value to development activities. This type of support has several advantages, particularly where individuals wish to be home-based learners or where they are geographically far-flung. Coombe and White (1994), for example, show how materials produced by groups of professionals in East African countries were successfully used in headteacher development and were supported by occasional group reflection opportunities with a practical focus. More commonly, 15 of the 96 KEEP survey schools were, in 1995, using Open University materials to support their CPD work, with several individuals also following newly developed distance-learning programmes being offered by other HE institutions.

Most distance-learning activities involve the production of localized research focused around school development and as such provide examples of an action research focus where participants plan, implement, record and evaluate change. Bayne-Jardine and Holly (1994) stress the participative nature of working partnerships which bypass hierarchical structures. While this is advantageous, work deemed to be 'research' is not always seen as a 'real' feature of daily school life.

The links between research-based investigations and classroom practice are fundamental if professional development is to be of any lasting value (Elliott, 1991b). In response to this, and also as part of a growth from school-based research, the potential of collaborative activities for development in both curriculum and pedagogy is now being recognized to the point that schools are beginning to provide time and support for mutual observation, work shadowing and mentoring.

Observation

Teachers are increasingly being encouraged to observe each other in the classroom, both formally and informally 'as a spin off from appraisal processes and the development of shared working in so many school activities'. This trend has, consequently, helped to promote the evaluation of both classroom management and teaching and learning. For example, in one case study school the staff are allocated one day each year to undertake observational activities with colleagues of their choice on condition that during the subsequent week reflective discussions take place, using a structure developed on the basis of experience as well as a proforma to guide the process. Staff are observed by their headteacher in two case study schools as part of an ongoing programme of review, although it is conceded that the process of in-class observation needs careful handling since it can too easily appear to lack the qualities of mutuality and joint activity which characterize much of the shared observation work increasingly evident, for example, in primary schools. Five of the 40 primary schools in the 1995 cohort comment on the way in which such professional development has fostered staff confidence and willingness to share developmental work.

Work-shadowing

This development has grown out of the need to provide management development opportunities for middle managers and those aspiring to senior management which 'show it like it is'. The problem is that the 'unreality' of the shadowing process may actually inhibit relationships and professional transactions between colleagues. Montgomery (1990) suggests that the value of shadowing is that it demonstrates a range of different management approaches to complex change situations and relationships which, if followed by a structured debriefing, may provide insights into the link between theory and practice.

Mentoring

While there have been considerable developments in mentoring as a support system for trainee teachers (Glover and Mardle, 1995; Wilkin and Sankey, 1994) increasing use is made of mentoring as both general and peer support for newly qualified teachers (NQTs) during induction, or for more experienced teachers undertaking additional or different responsibilities. Mentoring at an inservice level involves being 'a sort of prop if and when it's needed... but more importantly somebody with whom I could talk things over at the end of the day if I need it'. It is being used in a quarter of case study schools – most often where heads work with other heads.

Mentoring has also been useful for newly appointed heads of department (HODs). However, only one school we investigated could be described as offering an apparent 'mentoring culture' in which teachers use a mutual support system as a basis for reflection and as 'a boost to morale' within a climate of 'entitlement'. ap Thomas (1994), in an account of the ways that higher degree students utilize mentoring, stresses that a voluntary principle is vital for success and should include:

- minimum external organization;
- maximum choice for the mentor and mentee; and
- a clear connection between mentoring and school needs.

In your experience...

Try to identify a stage in your own career when the availability of a mentor might have been of help. How would you have wanted to use such a person? What potential problems might there be with this role?

Your responses to this question are likely to highlight the importance of relationships between people within groups or teams in a school or college and the importance of organizational culture. Mutuality, open constructive criticism, and shared values in achieving institutional aims appear to characterize schools where there has been a marked increase in internally developed and evaluated professional support systems.

Integrating Professional Practices

Discussions with staff in project schools and data from survey responses over several years suggests that staff are more ready to be open and adventurous in developing classroom-based activities where both ITE and appraisal are well developed within an organization and encourage a greater flexibility of approach and a more reflective attitude.

Initial Teacher Education and Professional Development

Each of the case study schools in the KEEP project is involved with either a local college of higher education or a university department offering teacher education. These evolving partnerships in ITE are indicative of changes to previous arrangements where students were often 'placed' in schools for training. Following the publication of Circular 9/92 (DES, 1992) HEIs were required to arrange for up to 66 per cent of the ITT year to be undertaken in schools, with the clear implication that much of the enhanced teacher education role would be undertaken by school staff.

Although mentoring training in relation to this enhanced role was often regarded as inadequate within case study schools, PDCs nevertheless valued the opportunities provided in supervising trainee teachers. One of them comments that this has prompted:

> all sorts of ways of reconsidering how we do things in class – a real awareness that our associates [trainee teachers] can bring us new ideas which are worth consideration... and an extra pair of hands so that we can explore alternative ways of doing things.

Indeed, one member of staff for whom no trainee teacher was available expressed great disappointment, because 'I'd undertaken the mentor training seriously – and I know that the pupils I taught with a student [trainee teacher] had gained so much more'.

The organization of teacher training is managed and organized in many schools by someone other than the PDC. As one deputy head comments, this tends to give 'messages to staff that initial teacher training is a separate function for which people are paid separately, and as such it represents a bit of a lost opportunity'. Only three of the 56 secondary schools in the 1995 survey used the same member of staff to manage all its staff development functions. Nevertheless, interview evidence shows that eight of the 12 case study schools have joint planning groups or their equivalent, showing at least some awareness of the way in which different staff needs can be met through a full range of opportunities.

Appraisal and Professional Development

Appraisal is increasingly used as a way of identifying the professional development needs of individual staff. Survey data from 1993 revealed that it was used as part of the process in 30 per cent of the schools questioned, but within two years has become a planning instrument in 94 per cent of responding secondary and 56 per cent of responding primary schools. The importance of appraisal to identify 'what individual staff feel they need, and for guiding the PDC's planning... for notifying people of opportunities' is widely acknowledged, but in about half of the schools investigated in some detail, it is also seen by senior managers as 'a reflective process which by asking staff to think about their work enables them to develop strategies by which we can jointly manage changes'. Used in this latter sense, it can be a means of staff development: several members of staff in project schools say how much they appreciate a colleague's support – 'having another angle on what you're doing is important, but only when you can trust their judgement' – and,

> having somebody come in and observe three lessons... and then discuss things with me... it's good having the chance to put things a bit more into context... how it fits in with the department and the school's approach... at least it's establishing some kind of common basis... some common support.

Copley and Thomas (1995), reviewing the process in one school argue, however, that the needs identification process is, of itself, often insufficient and that follow-up is essential or else staff feel it to be a wasted process. In their investigation, only 17 per cent of the staff who had been appraised felt they had gained the support which had been identified.

Competences and Professional Development

One headteacher also comments that targets arising from appraisal are 'becoming increasingly concerned with what *has* to be achieved to fare well in the promotion stakes'. This view has been accentuated, especially within senior school management, by the relatively recent introduction of competence-based approaches to training and the government's focus on management training at different career stages. Ouston (1993) and Eraut (1993) set out the theoretical basis for this and suggest that school effectiveness may be enhanced if, first, the necessary competences can be identified, and second, they are then developed in individuals aspiring to management and leadership. McCann (1994) has extended the applicability of this approach to NQTs, and Thomas (1994) has shown how understanding a set of competences can be fundamental to staff development within an LEA.

Hamlin (1990) and Earley (1991) outline alternative competence schemes, while Green (1991) outlines the work of a national assessment centre developing competences such as problem analysis, sensitivity and stress tolerance. The considerable body of literature on competence development suggests that a variety of strategies, including courses, consultancy and distance learning/mentoring, are increasingly likely to be used for developing the specific skills and understanding which the government and TTA, for example, see as crucial professional requirements. Nevertheless, there is also some disquiet about the applicability of competence-based approaches within educational settings (Ecclestone, 1995).

Professional Development Planning

Interview evidence from the case study schools shows that there is also an increasing tendency to develop an approach to professional development planning which utilizes both formal and informal structures as opportunities for staff. For example, one school notes that,

> we provided around 300 hours of staff development activity... a review of progress in curriculum plans, individual time for planning and materials development, skills development in information technology and science especially... and so much more – actually at very little cost to the school

because we planned it into an examination period – but with an enormous gain because staff felt that they'd been given something.

The professional development policy and planning structures developed in another case study school attempt to guarantee continuing development opportunities. The school's annual CPD programme as published in 1994 is outlined in Box 2.1.

Box 2.1: Professional development programme

September	Induction day for new staff
	Departmental review day
October	Staff conference
	– day one: school topics
	– day two: individual topics
November	School planning review evening
	School planning review at departmental and year meetings
December	Mentor introduction for ITE
January	Extended school experience for trainees/mentors (to March)
	School planning proposals at staff meetings
February	Appraisal cycle begins
March	Departmental planning meetings
April	PDC interviews with HODs – budget preparation
May	Individual PD staff time allocated
June	Appraisal reviews
July	End of year staff conference

In your experience…

Is this programme typical of what your own institution provides, or does it exist in another form? What opportunities for development and training might have been missed by the PDC concerned?

Your responses will provide a review of the features of your own environment and an opportunity for reflection on the way in which CPD is organized in your school or college. This information should be retained for use when you consider related issues in later chapters.

In assessing the value of professional development activities, many staff commented on the value of networks to better inform policy and planning development – 'those planning and working groups which we used to be part of when teachers' centres were curriculum and social meeting places'. The importance of subject-based groups has been recognized by the examination boards and 'we now find that the exam board meetings are a way of working with others and swapping stories about practice within different schools'. Mentoring also provides opportunities for joint planning and development activities between staff within ITE partnerships and there is an increasing interest amongst PDCs in linking with colleagues in similar roles in other institutions to allow an exchange of 'know-how'. The grant-maintained schools network has been effective in this respect – to some degree through force of circumstance.

One of the effects of the growth of better planned inservice activities has been that working parties and group activities within schools are increasingly important means of cross-curricular development with a consequent 'strengthening of mutual support in planning things for the good of the school'. One headteacher involved in the KEEP research argues that 'quite simply, as the culture develops, the demands get greater and planning is even more important'. PDCs identify three needs if a development culture is to be positively encouraged and 'owned' by staff. The PDC in one school speaks for several when he points out that:

> It's a matter of planning to be flexible… firstly, taking opportunities when we can use them, then secondly, evaluating them as positive aids to developing both our staff and the school, and then *finally*, recording what has been taking place so that each individual, each one of us, has what is becoming a continuing record of our plans and targets – and any attempts we've made to reach them.

In this particular school, reassurances given about confidentiality in appraisal have meant that the detail is only available to the PDC if staff wish to give it and, in addition, the school highlights the need for *all* staff to take the opportunity of being involved in planning and management processes.

If professional development is to be an integrated and coherent force in improving both teacher and then organizational performance, it is crucial that each institution determines its own policy framework within the broader national context. For most institutions, the key elements in determining and formulating institutional policy can be summarized under three headings:

1. *The parameters*: there needs to be an agreed and preferably shared consensus about what counts as continuing professional development: how does the institution define CPD?

2. *The structures*: there is a need for clarity and transparency in professional development structures and organization.
3. *The personnel*: any contributory roles and responsibilities need to be clear and communicated to all staff.

Hewton (1988) in considering staff development policy-making, suggests that the acronym ASPECT illustrates the key elements involved:

Aims: what are the purposes of staff development?
Structure: who is responsible and in what ways?
Programme: what kind of provision should be available?
Evaluation: how and when will review take place and who will do it and present the results?
Cost: what are the resource implications of CPD?
Timing: what can realistically be achieved within the agreed timescale and what should take priority?

Managing Shared Decision-making

The development of a workable and effective policy is often reliant on a sense of shared decision-making – also a frequently cited key aspect in the process of managing effective change. This issue is explored by Fullan (1991; 1993) and illustrated as a fundamental part of successful development work by Hargreaves and Hopkins (1991). Our evidence suggests that although greater staff involvement is developing within both primary and secondary schools, professional development opportunities remain, in many institutions, either unplanned and haphazard, or alternatively overly authoritatively planned and offered with little or no meaningful consultation. Tables 2.1 and 2.2 illustrate the range of planning and decision-making arrangements for formal CPD opportunities within primary and secondary schools respectively, derived from the 1995 survey.

The size and structure of management teams within each school may explain the degree to which professional development committees and senior management teams are used as principal decision-makers – especially for whole-school activities. It is significant, however, that in a quarter of case study schools professional development programme planning follows on from school development planning, since,

> once the priorities for our development plan are set we're in a situation
> where all decision-making about resources is made much easier, and training
> is one of these... if we know where we are going then we can try to match up
> what people say they want – within the limits of our available budget, which
> is tight.

44

Table 2.1 *Consultation processes in relation to continuing professional development (56 secondary schools, 1995)*

Process	Whole school development	Departmental development	Individual development
Staff consultation on proposals	5	1	
Staff discussions to develop ideas	5	7	
SDP led and priorities set	16	10	
PDC initiated	4	6	9
Professional development committee planning	10	4	3
Senior management team proposes/approves	13	9	5
Head and/or deputy proposes/ approves	3	5	4
Line management and appraisal proposal			24
Personal initiative and request			12

There is a tendency in the primary sector for all teaching staff to be more actively involved in discussions about appropriate CPD activities, especially where 'as a team in everything that we do we really don't see a difference between making decisions about what's worthwhile training and making decisions about curriculum issues and the resources we have in school'.

Table 2.2 *Decision-making for continuing professional development (37 primary schools, 1995 – three schools declined to answer this question)*

School size: number on roll	Whole staff decision	Senior management decision	Headteacher decision
85–200	4	3	3
201–300	4	5	1
301–400	1	7	1
401–520	–	8	–
Total	9	23	5

Table 2.2 indicates the tendency for smaller schools to rely on collegial approaches to decision-making regarding course attendance and which INSET topics should be prioritized, eg, whole-staff gatherings as well as established one-to-one relationships between individuals and the head to determine priorities. Larger schools appear to make greater use of increasingly

sophisticated approaches, including annual needs audits, individual questionnaires and, in a minority of primary schools, external adviser assessments as
part of the LEA's servicing package.

In your experience...

*Consider the way in which decisions are made concerning the pattern of involvement in the
various professional development activities within your organization. What criteria are used
in the process?*

It is likely that the decision-making process in your institution fits somewhere
along a continuum from a totally randomized, submission-by-submission
decision-making process, to a system which works towards an annual programme of individual, departmental or team and whole-school activities based
on known criteria and related to the overall development of the organization.
In some schools, however, the criteria are not known and staff resent the
apparent 'ad hockery' of decision-making.

All responding secondary schools in 1995 say they made some use of their
School Development Plan (SDP), with 92 per cent saying they use information
from appraisal and departmental development plans to plan activities. This
contrasts with the less optimistic investigation conducted by MORI for the
TTA (Page and Fisher-Jones, 1995), but may reflect the possibility that our
sample of responding schools was more reliant on senior managers and PDCs
as respondents, who may be more motivated to report positive rather than
negative experiences and developments. Teachers in project schools tended
to see a more limited linkage between appraisal and development planning.

Only 50 per cent of responding schools actually produce a PDP as a separate
document, which may be a comment on the variability in quality of school
development planning as instanced by Levacic and Glover (1994). Their
assessment of the use made of rational planning by OFSTED inspectors found
that 80 per cent of the schools inspected had deficiencies in development
plans. This was mainly because staff development needs and the consequent
costings had not been investigated within school planning processes. While it
seems that separate SDPs and PDPs are not formally required, training and
development requirements still need to be identified. This is in addition to a
statement about associated costs and the evaluation criteria to be used in
judging success.

Within the primary schools sector, there is a tendency for larger schools to
use appraisal and SDPs to guide formal professional development documen-

tation. It seems, however, that greater uniformity of practice is more closely related to LEA guidance and advice than it is to overall school size. A separate PDP existed in only 25 per cent of the primary schools.

Some staff in case study schools expressed concern that the system is 'too bound to the development plan with a real risk that when anything worthwhile comes along either for individuals or for a group of staff, we may not be able to fund participation'. Development planning requires forward planning over a two to three year minimum period and it may be that greater flexibility is needed to meet unforeseen opportunities and contingencies so that developments are not overly rigid.

Wallace (1991) argues that annual reviews provide opportunities for replanning in order to meet a restricted number of clear objectives, while Harding (1995) shows how known and established planning routines clearly linking aims, resource base and necessary inservice are more likely to succeed. For one school, a crucial rule has been identified: 'unless the activity is linked to a development plan objective then, whatever the emergency, it can't be done this year!'

Reflection...

In many schools decision-making for professional development has become more open, involving the staff as a whole, even though budgetary allocation of resources may still be subject to closed negotiation. Why does this occur? Does it necessarily reflect senior management attitudes to INSET?

You and your colleagues may consider that attitudes to CPD decision-making have changed over recent years as new structures, newly developed skills and funding relationships have had an impact. Our project evidence suggests there has been a marked change in approaches to professional development management and development planning between 1993 and 1995.

While this may follow growing administrative skills in relation to local financial management, it may also be related to moves towards more open management approaches resulting from legal requirements for the publication of data and greater staff involvement in development planning. These changes may signal alterations in overall senior management attitudes, particularly evident amongst newer and younger headteachers, to human resource management. For example, it is significant that only three of the case study schools showed any evidence that headteachers define precisely directed time for staff development activities – a marked decline from the proportion evident in 1993.

This kind of situation may also reflect the spread of more collegial management techniques and/or a greater willingness amongst senior staff to delegate the management of professional development to other staff. Whatever the reason, a shift from LEA-managed professional development to greater institutional autonomy and site-based management offers opportunities for greater staff involvement – an important element in their professional lives. Pressures on time and restricted funding still exist, however, and managing these issues is likely to remain with senior staff, given the potential for conflict.

Managing the Tensions and Achieving a Balance

The most significant tension identified by survey schools concerns the important link between appraisal and CPD – a linkage which has led to expectations which most schools find difficult to sustain. Two kinds of balance need to be maintained:

1. *The focus* – the balance between the demands of the whole institution, its departments or teams, and the individuals who work there, so as to maintain a sense of equity.
2. *The means* – the balance concerning different types of provision to ensure that a spread of activities is offered so that as many needs as possible are met.

Table 2.1 has already shown how, within larger schools, decision-making tends to occur at three levels, reflecting a need for balance where, for example,

> we would expect the staff as a whole would want some say on the topics being included in our annual inservice programme – and that they would want to express a view about the most effective ways in which we can deal with these topics... but departments have a clearer idea of their own needs... and these do vary from group to group – and, of course, individuals *must* be given an opportunity to express what are essentially personal needs.

The way schools utilize their budgets often reflects differing philosophies. For example, one respondent points out that 'we're having to learn that we have considerable potential for staff training within the school and that we can't embark on expensive courses with even more costly supply staff'. By contrast, another comments that 'we need to buy good value courses if we are to help staff feel inspired for change'. One school spends all its resources on 'the actual costs of provision for people – we have a deliberate policy of using the money for this – and avoiding the use of supply cover which is an enormous drain on professional development funds'. Table 2.3 shows the range and average percentages of expenditure on key INSET elements under the main INSET/ PD headings, but excludes the costs of appraisal.

Table 2.3 *Spending on continuing professional development: the key elements in 96 primary and secondary schools, 1995*

Area of expenditure	Range %	Median %
Speakers	1–30	12
Course fees	5–80	40
Supply staff	10–90	45
Hospitality	0–20	5

An indication of the demand on resources is shown by the fact that 15 per cent of secondary schools spend between 1 per cent and 11 per cent on travel. Further questioning reveals that some of this money is used to meet staff travel claims for a range of 'semi-linked' purposes, in other words, virement without real acknowledgement that this is occurring. Of these schools, most are rural and while some are urban, they are distant from their county town. GM schools continue to mention travel costs as important for maintaining networks where for example, local LEA provision is 'not welcoming to our staff'. A quarter of schools use some of their funding (varying between 5 per cent and 30 per cent) to purchase books and staff development materials, with high spending being defended because 'we use some of our funds for curriculum materials for departmental use as a way of helping staff to become more effective'.

Perhaps not surprisingly, it proved difficult to identify the proportion of funding being spent on each of the three areas of staff development – whole-school, departmental and individual development. Several schools point to an 'interrelationship between the three which may be false and which may indicate a separateness which doesn't exist'. Table 2.4 shows the range and median expenditure patterns of secondary schools, suggesting that they may be moving towards a more balanced provision. As one PDC comments,

> we believe that all the work has to have a whole-school origin, which is then worked on by departments and which highlights the need for individual knowledge and skills training – really there is no alternative to a single approach.

Table 2.4 *Spending on continuing professional development: areas of focus*
(56 secondary schools, 1995)

Area of development	Range %	Median %
Whole-school development	10–95	30
Departmental development	15–80	50
Individual development	5–30	20

Our research data suggest that secondary schools are, in general, spending about 30 per cent of their resources on whole-school developments, 50 per cent on departmental needs (mainly to meet National Curriculum implementation), and the remaining 20 per cent being allocated for individual development. In the primary sector, the concentration of resources on whole school needs is 80 per cent, with the remaining 20 per cent linking subject specialism and individual needs.

Identifying and Analysing Needs

Needs analysis is fundamental to any decision-making process. It is crucial that the differing perspectives taken by the various groups and individuals are recognized and considered in the needs identification process if real institutional improvement is to be derived from professional development. Fullan (1990) asserts the need for teachers' personal and professional lives to be viewed holistically, while Oldroyd and Hall (1991) argue that needs identification 'is a valuable INSET activity in its own right. Properly handled, it can promote professional reflection... particularly when it is linked to and raises awareness about school and curriculum review and development plans'.

Caldwell and Spinks' focus (1988) on 'self-managing' schools has encouraged the trend towards identifying school priorities based on assessments of its various resource needs for organizing particular aspects of the curriculum. One case study school has underpinned its activities with these principles and then used its SDP as a driving force for professional development. Aims and objectives for each part of the CPD programme are linked to resource implications, including individual staff development and training needs. For example Box 2.2 shows how the two interrelate.

Box 2.2: Personal and social education

Aim	To increase understanding of the courts system
Objective	Role play to identify the principal personnel, procedures and powers of the magistrates' courts
Time	One lesson preparation, one lesson activity, one lesson debriefing
Costs/ materials	Materials: Class sets @ £3.50 per group Video: 'The Sentence of the Courts' @ £10.00
Staff implications	AJ as lead teacher to spend one morning familiarization at the courts – £45 Planning session for all tutors in Yr 10 groups – October meeting time

---

In this way, planning is driven by curriculum needs. The starting point in another school is an assessment by members of staff of specific needs which will enable them to cope adequately with the following years' teaching programme. This strategy has the advantage of being 'a response by the staff to their own needs... we ask them to relate it to our general targets established at appraisal'. However, there are also limitations 'where we know of whole-school needs which the individual assessment will not be interested in... as a result some of the annual programme appears to be top down'.

Trimble (1993) examines a primary school's staff development policy, arguing that needs analysis should not be about weaknesses or problems but should instead focus on developing the necessary skills to 'boost morale, increase job satisfaction, improve productivity, and ultimately make the way children learn more effective'. A potential danger in linking INSET and appraisal is that development may appear to be too readily related to individual shortcomings. Where a positive organizational culture exists which includes shared needs identification, planning and prioritization, development is more closely linked with personal professional growth, although meeting demands still frequently requires the allocation of scarce resources, with all the attendant difficulties.

Managing Resources: The Professional Development Budget

Schools reporting in the 1995 primary and secondary surveys indicated which members of their staff were responsible for constructing and managing their professional development budgets. As the delegation of funds continues, schools need to manage professional development as a resource and while 80 per cent of secondary schools report that bursars (or their equivalent) undertake the budgeting role, it remains the responsibility of primary headteachers in all except the largest schools. The TTA survey (Page and Fisher-Jones, 1995) also notes that heads who control INSET budgets tend to deploy funds in a different way from PDCs – making greater use of staff as in-house trainers, for example, rather than employing outside experts or consultants.

Funding and budgeting issues across Europe tend to have a somewhat different focus. CPD is, under most circumstances, a voluntary activity within most European countries, although in certain cases INSET becomes a formal requirement. In Spain, for example, CPD is obligatory for those seeking promotion with staff being released for up to eight days a year – provided they can prove that CPD is not otherwise available and that replacement teaching and cover will be undertaken by school staff. Although schools elsewhere in Europe are generally not concerned with funding, the issue of time is still clearly important.

Reflection...

How far would a scheme like the one operating in Spain be appropriate within a British context? Would it benefit the teaching profession?

You may have found that two particular viewpoints emerge here. There is the argument that financial budgeting gives schools greater freedom to determine who participates in which courses and activities. Another view is that rights offered as part of the conditions of service will ensure the provision of development opportunities. This latter approach may well obviate the need for bargaining within increasingly autonomous management of institutions. While schools in the UK maintain the voluntary principle for personal development, there is also increasing pressure – often justified as part of directed time – to identify development activities as part of the meetings programme. Nevertheless, both compulsory and voluntary elements require funding.

Work with KEEP schools points to the existence of a continuum of budgetary practice. For example, at one end the funds in one school are delegated to the deputy head responsible for personnel who then allocates them on the basis of requests in a pragmatic manner, since 'we generally have enough to last the year, but if staff get a bit too heavy in their demands it may be a matter of saying that we can't help'. At the other end of the continuum in another school, the planned budget is based on a review of all staff requests before any decisions are made, with the consequent understanding that 'we just can't meet any late requests – although there is a small contingency fund'. Overall our investigations show three kinds of CPD budget allocation procedures are being used.

1. *Historic budgeting* – where sums used in the previous year are adjusted, eg, according to inflation, and used as a framework for the coming year.
2. *Zero-based budgeting* – where all possible professional development participants are asked to submit requests based on perceived needs, starting from zero each year.
3. *Programme-based budgeting* – where the constituent parts of the school development programme are costed and then prioritized so that demands can be matched with possible income.

Of these three procedures, programme-based budgeting is, in essence, the approach most likely to be driven by the institution's needs. However, the management process can become complicated, particularly when professional development resources are devolved to groups of staff or 'programmes' and each individual aspect of a school's CPD programme is evaluated independently rather than as part of the total INSET budget.

Although CPD funding has only relatively recently been delegated to schools in the UK, a variety of budgetary strategies and allocation processes exist. These may be a combination of LEA advice, recent historical precedent, personal idiosyncrasy and perceptions about best practice. Consider the cameo in Box 2.3.

Box 2.3: Funding CPD

Green School… a secondary school with 720 students, has a total CPD budget allocation of £17,300, which is managed by the deputy head (personnel). The annual programme of INSET days is whole-school focused and involves buying-in three days of consultancy. Departments are then allocated supply days so that they can have a full day of INSET during the summer term each year. Remaining funds are used to support individual requests for attendance at courses etc., or

---

for supply days to undertake specified work, or to allow some payment towards the fees for longer courses. Any under- or overspend is carried forward each year.

Taylor's School... a secondary school of similar size, has a total CPD budget allocation of £13,500, but has used £3,900 of this to buy into an LEA support scheme. The PDC then asks for submissions from the senior management team, departments, the deputy in charge of appraisal, and individual staff in order to build up an annual programme. All submissions are openly prioritized according to the development plan and these data are then discussed with the local adviser to determine how much help the LEA support agreement can provide. No carry forward is allowed.

Reflection...

Given these admittedly sketchy outlines, which process do you consider is likely to be more effective in meeting overall institutional aims?

You may well conclude that Taylor's has a more effective system because it uses its resources for identified whole-school objectives. One of the staff in the school, however, has commented that,

> our system makes us submit details which we can't really know about some months before the event... courses are usually published about a term in advance and we might not need supply help if we're able to negotiate involvement when its a lighter timetable day... and then there's the need to be able to respond quickly when something, say a problem, comes up.

Taylor's has met this difficulty by allowing planning submissions to include notional figures for course fees, travel and supply based on the unit average from the previous year. The school's professional development culture is demonstrated, however, in the reaction that 'the actual figures balance out in the course of the year... we really want to know what benefits development activities bring and how staff will evaluate what they've done after the event'.

Part of this general problem stems from the fact that painstaking course and activity evaluations may result in very full – and potentially cumbersome – school records, which are then needed for future planning. Our research evidence suggests, however, that PDCs are under so much pressure that planning informed by past evaluations may not be a realistic and practical possibility at present. It is, then, a question of balance. The need is for sufficient information for planning, but not so much that planning is inhibited. In their summary report of the TTA survey, Page and Fisher-Jones (1995) conclude that 'more efforts to encourage schools to assess carefully the CPD activities staff are involved in, should pay dividends in terms of improved classroom success' (p.7).

Changing Roles and Responsibilities: The PDC

The increase in professional development activities and the growing recognition of their potential impact on school improvement has resulted in what is effectively becoming a new senior management role. In 1993, 70 per cent of the schools contributing to our research had a designated professional development coordinator (PDC). By 1995, this role was recognized in 97 per cent of responding secondary schools. Warwick (1975) has argued that neither headteachers nor deputies are the best professionals to undertake a PDC's responsibilities since the degree of informality and counselling skills required are incongruous with their management status and role. However, this concern over potential incompatibility has not been borne out in recent developments. In effect, practices vary according to management structures and previous experiences. For example, in the 1995 survey a deputy head coordinated INSET/CPD functions in 76 per cent of secondary schools; in 8 per cent it was coordinated through a senior teacher with personnel responsibilities; in 12 per cent through a head of department, while it is apparently managed in 4 per cent of schools through negotiations between separately designated INSET and CPD staff.

Interview evidence also suggests that there is a progressive gathering together of personnel functions as senior management rationalization takes place, and as the proportion of deputy heads undertaking professional development responsibilities increases. This may have 'facilitated administration but if the burden on the deputy is too great, it will have done nothing to improve the philosophy behind professional development'. The TTA survey (Page and Fisher-Jones, 1995) suggests there is a link between planning and coordination responsibilities, noting that schools with PDCs were 'more likely to have a planned programme than where a head of deputy takes responsibility'. Our evidence supports this assertion to some extent, but in two case study schools highly successful CPD is managed by deputy heads who have responsibility for all aspects of human resource management.

In your experience...

How far has the professional development role within your organization been developed as a positive response to changing need? What do you regard as the 'person specification' for such a role?

It may be that your PDC has taken an increasingly central role in your organization, reflecting a growing focus on development activities and the need to see INSET as a strategic concern. Alternatively, the post-holder may be relatively invisible in your institution, the role may have unclear parameters, and the responsibilities may be relatively undervalued. It is useful to consider how far the public image of the PDC reflects the impact that professional development itself has on your institution and how far the two are linked.

Our evaluation of KEEP data indicates that PDCs need to deal with most or all of the following tasks:

- *managing information* (receiving and distributing);
- *managing programme planning* (consultation with decision-makers);
- *managing programme implementation* (liaison with providers, local arrangements, publicity);
- *matching whole-school, departmental and individual needs* (the potential appraisal link);
- *overseeing financial management and control*; and
- *facilitating involvement through administrative arrangements* (eg, supply cover arrangements).

Clearly, however, the role is evolving. When PDCs were asked which training and development opportunities they needed to match their enhanced role, they repeatedly requested support in developing counselling skills: 'to be used when I have the time to work with individuals'; and budget management skills: 'in order to develop the best way of handling resources'.

While two-thirds of those managing professional development overall were male, there is no direct evidence that the role is gender-related, except in so far as senior management posts are, historically, more likely to be held by men. Twenty-five per cent of schools were paying an extra allowance to staff taking responsibility for professional development, but only two deputy heads came into this group – and one of those appears to get additional remuneration for an ITE mentoring role within an HEI-school partnership arrangement.

Professional development for PDCs is usually very limited and generally 'the product of day courses at LEA level – it's more for administration than to understand the background to professional development'. Nevertheless, two PDCs had participated in longer courses leading to a Professional Development Certificate – a fact reflected in the apparently more integrated approach to INSET management evident in their schools. In addition, a further two PDCs had undertaken some personnel-related work as part of a Masters degree course.

Overall, it appears that only half of those managing professional development have had any form of training or development related to their role, with only 8 per cent of the INSET which had been undertaken being 'conceptual' in a way which would enhance the quality of CPD policy development as well as support a more informed CPD institutional philosophy. While INSET opportunities focused on 'nuts and bolts', there was no clear evidence that it supported fully the development of excellence in practice which stresses an integrated approach with aspects of school life. It may be that the development of accredited school-based activities will enhance professional development and training opportunities for PDCs and that the informal networks which are developing amongst both LEA and GM school networks may improve the skills base for this aspect of personnel management. One headteacher comments that,

> if appraisal is to have credibility, and if initial teacher education is to provide identified opportunities, then we need to give our responsible staff the time to reflect on their role, on the needs of the people they manage, and on the reality of development against a declining resource base.

The evidence from the staff interviewed alongside responses from the survey schools indicates that one of the most important skills required by those managing inservice education and training is the ability to negotiate in order to 'select, employ and evaluate what is being offered, so that we can satisfy the needs of the staff and ensure the development of the school'. For this to happen effectively, both PDCs and the staff in schools need to have a greater awareness of the strengths and weaknesses of a growing and diversified pool of providers.

CHAPTER 3

Privatization, Priorities and Professional Development

Determining Priorities

As Chapter 1 made clear, our investigations have taken place during a period of considerable change within education. Initially, following the 1988 Education Act, inservice education in schools was largely driven by the need to adapt rapidly to meet National Curriculum teaching and assessment requirements. LEAs frequently utilized a cascade model of introducing change by offering courses on an authority-wide basis, while other providers also offered a good deal of 'mass' training. Although government funding was made available to support schools and LEAs in meeting newly detailed national objectives, the UK has never had a centrally imposed pattern of training which *must* be undertaken by some or all staff. Decisions over participation in particular programmes has, instead, rested with individual staff, managers and fund-holders. This contrasts with a European-wide developing pattern of setting national target areas for INSET. In 1994, for example, the Italian government required primary schools to be involved in centrally organized and locally provided training for the teaching of auditory, music, artistic and motor skills – though this fact alone is not indicative of the quality of the provision.

By 1991, the devolution of GEST funding to schools in England and Wales and the development of prioritized training objectives had resulted in the development of an increasingly coherent approach to CPD for all secondary schools and most primary schools. The freedom to make budgets according to school needs following the introduction of LMS has resulted in varying amounts of additional funding being used in support where GEST has been considered insufficient. This has gradually shifted the purchasing power within an embryonic INSET marketplace to schools as they initiate professional development programmes to meet needs which are both identifiably broader in focus and yet more specific in context than previously. Survey results gathered over the past three years indicate several tendencies within secondary schools:

- *Diversified provision*: schools now offer more diverse CPD programmes which are increasingly based on their own self-evaluation of need.
- *Marketized provision*: courses and conferences as offered by LEAs are no longer regarded by schools as either sufficient or wholly appropriate for their needs.
- *Individualized provision*: the introduction of OFSTED inspection and greater institutional autonomy has meant that CPD activities are increasingly driven by the need to respond to a variety of external and internal pressures, each of which varies in impact according to the individual institutional context.

While these tendencies are also evident within the primary sector, albeit to a lesser degree, there is greater reticence in this phase to use what is generally more limited purchasing power to go beyond LEA provision, since 'we already have a good LEA service into which we buy and which meets most of our needs as they can plan for schools in general'. Furthermore, 'we have neither the time nor the inclination to get involved in seeking out services when we know that the LEA does its best for us'. While such comments may arguably reflect the remnants of benevolent paternalism in the LEA-primary school relationships, the programmes offered in (or for) primary schools nevertheless tend to be more communal and uniform, with whole groups or clusters of schools working together and moving along similar lines of development. LEAs can, therefore, be a cost-effective facilitator and focus for networking for primary schools.

In your experience...

How far has the professional development programme offered in your institution during the past year been indicative of the kinds of internal and external pressures which you feel staff have been facing? How far should it reflect a concern with relatively immediate imperatives rather than focusing on longer-term development needs?

The range of topics you are likely to have identified as key elements in your institution's INSET programme will probably fall into the following broad categories:

- national policy implementation;
- curriculum development to meet pupil needs; and
- process skills to enhance management of the learning environment.

You will notice that the external pressures are being interpreted from the particular response of each school, but that common threads of teaching and learning run through all programmes.

Tables 3.1 and 3.2 show how far these elements were found in responding schools and outlines the areas prioritized by primary and secondary schools for professional development during 1995.

Table 3.1 *Priorities for professional development in primary schools, 1995 (40 schools)*

Ranking	NC content	Appraisal	Inspection	Management	NC assessment	SEN	Development planning	Cross-curricular
1–2	23	2	4	8	8	10	12	3
3–4	5	6	2	8	9	9	4	7
5–6	–	2	3	5	4	5	3	4
7–8	7	8	10	4	5	5	6	5
All	35	18	19	25	26	29	25	19

Table 3.2 *Priorities for professional development in secondary schools, 1995 (54 schools)*

Ranking	NC content	Appraisal	Inspection	Management	NC assessment	SEN	Development planning	Cross-curricular
1–2	31	–	17	14	20	9	13	2
3–4	5	11	8	15	8	16	4	3
5–6	2	7	2	9	4	8	8	5
7–8	3	7	5	3	1	2	3	11
Total	41	25	32	41	33	35	28	21

Compared with 1993 and 1994, the primary school figures illustrate the move from externally imposed topic programmes such as was evident during the first years of National Curriculum implementation, to a more mixed set of objectives. National Curriculum content and assessment topics continue to be seen as important during the post-Dearing period, but as appraisal and inspection preparation have been undertaken by many primary schools, their emphasis has shifted towards more internally driven development foci including generic management skills and planning.

The importance attaching to special educational needs (SEN) may still be a reaction to the 1994 legislation establishing the SEN code of practice, as schools endeavour to establish policies. The range of other topics includes both information technology and behaviour management mentioned in 10 per cent of responding schools. Also important are aspects of personal and social education, suggesting that this aspect of cross-curricular development is now being addressed within the larger primary schools. The move towards internal rather than external pressures is also illustrated by the spread of topics.

While National Curriculum content and the demands of the Dearing review remain a major concern in secondary schools, the pattern during 1995 reflects a greater diversity of programming. Although until recently National Curriculum assessment, inspection and appraisal dominated, the fact that these are now in place has brought a move towards topics of broader concern, including SEN, management issues and school development planning. The PDC in one case study school argued that,

> we need to have a diverse programme so that the staff have an opportunity for a degree of 'pick-and-mix' in order to feel that what they've done meets their own personal needs – or those of the department – as well as our objectives at the whole-school level.

More generally, headteachers and PDCs frequently point out the difficulties in prioritizing development topics easily because they may be the concern of only some staff. However, the impact of external pressures and a certain tenor of what might be called 'training instrumentalism' is clear. For example, 25 per cent of schools who attached importance to inspection were timetabled for OFSTED inspection at the time they were surveyed. The increased priority given to management and development issues does, however, suggest that once schools have been inspected, they rapidly move on to consider broader strategies for improvement and associated enhanced staff skills. Nevertheless, this initial pressure has sometimes enabled senior managers to sidestep potentially controversial prioritization issues, obviating the need to choose between individual staff INSET requests, particularly where funds are limited.

While our analysis concentrates on those topics regarded as most important, responding schools also listed other topics specific to their own circumstances. These fall into three categories, indicating that CPD is often interpreted within schools more broadly, rather than concentrating on the simple inculcation of necessary skills to facilitate effective curriculum delivery. This broader focus incorporates:

1. *A strategic perspective*, related to longer-term development planning and exemplified by concerns for marketing, for alternative post-16 opportunities, and for evaluating the institution's 'mission' – its aims and values.
2. *A skills perspective*, typified by a concern to develop and apply information technology and multimedia technology as a cross-institutional learning support – for both staff and students.

3. *A change perspective*, particularly in relation to teaching and learning and considered as whole-school issues and as part of the improvement process.

One PDC highlighted the continuing dilemma being faced when planning inservice programmes: though the distinction between developing knowledge, skills and attitude change, and meeting personal, departmental and whole-school objectives may often seem to be 'clear in the eyes of the person offering INSET, it's likely to be much less clear for us and for the teacher concerned... so we need to try to relate targets from both viewpoints'. The difficulties are illustrated in the vignettes in Box 3.1 (secondary school) and 3.2 (primary).

Box 3.1: The professional dilemma (secondary)

Arthur Jones is a 49-year-old English teacher, whose initial training had been in classics and who taught Latin full time until the grammar school in a large industrial town where he worked became a comprehensive high school in 1987. His 1995 appraisal targets included: '(a) the need to retrain so that I can teach A level English Literature; (b) the need to develop opportunities for Latin teaching as part of the English work; (c) work-shadowing one or more colleagues so that I can understand how to relate better to less-able pupils; (d) developing my counselling skills so that I improve my role as a group tutor'.

From the PDC's and headteacher's point of view, the real cost of this set of targets is seen as a minimum to be 'a part-time retraining opportunity which would mean one day a week at the local HEI for a term; a restructuring of the English curriculum which would take at least three days of departmental meetings; at least three days of supply cover each term to allow work-shadowing; and the time needed to attend the five-day counselling course at the LEA centre'. Their general comment in reviewing the targets was that, 'we can meet all these needs but there must be an understanding that, in the interests of the school, some prioritization is needed first'. Arthur Jones saw it, however, as 'yet another example of the way that they always say they'll do things for staff, but when it comes to it, they fail to deliver what we really need'.

Box 3.2: The professional dilemma (primary)

Joanne Johnson presented similar problems for her head who acted as PDC in a primary school with 87 pupils situated in a rural village in the Welsh Marches. Joanne had been a highly respected student at the college of higher education some 30 miles away and graduated with a first class honours degree. She then took up the post at her current school and became known for her expertise, developed over eight years, as a classroom teacher for Years 3 and 4 in a mixed group. Her skills in differentiated learning were noticed by a college tutor with whom she had worked mentoring student teachers over a period of five years. At the age of 30 she began an MA course specializing in curriculum studies. Mid-way through the course she approached her head with a request for greater responsibility in the school because, 'I think there's no real reason to move from working in an area and a school which I enjoy so much'.

From the head's point of view this suggestion is not really feasible because, with a staff of three, substantial changes in role are not really desirable. The head held the view that it would be in Joanna's best interests to establish herself elsewhere. While both parents and colleagues had frequently expressed confidence in what she was doing there was a growing expectation that she would 'want to move on to another challenge somewhere else'. Joanne regarded the failure to provide her with new opportunities and challenges as 'slap in the face' and a ploy on the part of the head and governors to move her elsewhere because, 'after all, I've become a threat to the head now and I suppose I'm getting too expensive for them'. She now felt embittered and demotivated.

These examples indicate how PDCs need both flexibility of approach and rapid access to detailed information regarding potential support mechanisms, and the time, financial and personal cost implications when planning ways of meeting staff development needs. Each of these dilemmas also highlights the way in which schools may need counselling support in helping their staff to meet their identified needs.

Negotiating in the INSET Marketplace

Legislation and changes in practice resulting from a more market-oriented education service mean that LEAs are no longer able to maintain advisory and inspection services which are invulnerable to market forces. With the delegation of budgets to schools, advisory services have often only remained viable where they have established 'service-level agreements'. Schools may contract to buy-in a package of advisory and course support, enabling a resulting transfer of funds back to the LEA so that existing services can continue. An alternative is to open LEA services to full market forces, requiring staff to self-fund their posts as part of an agency offering courses, conferences and consultancy to institutions able to buy in support.

Harland *et al.* (1993) have investigated the changes to LEA services during 1991 and 1992 and outline the impact of market awareness as a result of schools' developing discernment in selecting INSET services which best match their needs. They also trace the way in which such changes to the locus of control have promoted quality improvement within the service. Anderson (1991) and Bush *et al.* (1994) have shown that the grant-maintained sector has exerted great pressure for improvement in professional development services. This was achieved initially because INSET support was often denied to GM schools by parent LEAs, and subsequently because the buying power of these schools through the Special Purpose Grants (D) was often more than twice that of LEA schools of comparable size and type.

Although the early GM schools were often given substantial resources, they were also put in a market situation at an earlier stage than most LEA schools. The latter are increasingly aware of the need to secure the best possible return for their smaller budgets and have become similarly conscious of the need to optimize the value of available funds. Consequently, schools are increasingly concerned with issues of:

- *effectiveness* – the use of development activities to achieve the aims of the organization in a way which enhances the quality of learning and consequent outcomes;
- *efficiency* – the provision of effective activities at minimum cost considering the balance of human and physical resources; and
- *value for money* – the achievement of a balance between effective and efficient services and the amount of finance available to the school.

One PDC considers that 'effectiveness' involves:

taking on the sort of consultant who can present a good argument in a way which activates the thinking of everyone as a whole without causing us to feel patronized in any way – and who promotes the changes we really want to make.

Another sees 'efficiency' as:

achieving the maximum impact for the school at the sort of fees we can afford... and so if we manage our resources so there's an impact, then we may actually have got value for money... but really to be sure we'd have to evaluate what we're doing before we can really reach decisions of that sort.

In your experience...

Consider an INSET experience which you think has been effective, and one which you felt was efficient. What criteria could you use to assess value for money in these instances?

In considering these issues you may well have been seeking to establish some kind of system which enables you to make a comparison between what was wanted and what was achieved. To this end, classifying activities based on changes in knowledge, skills and attitude related to effective training and development methods may be valuable.

Joyce and Showers (1980) have argued that the acquisition of new skills may impact at one of four levels. These can be summarized as awareness; organized knowledge and theory; principles and skills; and the transfer of skills into the teaching repertoire. Activities selected may therefore have to meet pedagogic as well as organizational criteria. In one case study school, a planning sequence is followed (see Box 3.3) which provides a framework for providers as well as an assessment scheme for the school's managers 'so that we have real knowledge upon which to base choices for the future':

Box 3.3: Staff development planning submission

Proposed activity?	Half-day departmental meeting
Topic/focus?	Health and safety
Possible support and likely cost?	LEA adviser (TD) – known but limited, £80 Consultant (AF) – not known, but has good reputation, £100
Preferred provider?	Consultant (AF)
Criteria?	Process – departmental awareness of health and safety issues in physics labs Outcomes – change in policy document; change in practical lesson organization procedures; nil incident return after one year
Achievement?	New policy document to be written (one term) New procedures to operate in following year (under discussion) Three accidents with heat sources to be investigated (before half term)
Initial review? (HOD or DH)	HOD comment: Consultant good overall... but rather 'do as I say' instead of sharing people's concerns

---

The school concerned has now further refined its processes in action planning activities by developing INSET for all its middle managers after examining and negotiating the contract with several providers. The negotiation process involves four stages:

1. *Setting parameters*, through constructing the outline activity and developing a CPD 'brief', setting out aims and objectives, criteria for success, requirements for delivery, materials to be used etc.
2. *Implementing ideas,* through detailing the implementation process, including a clarification of the training/development approaches to be used and the nature of participant involvement.
3. *Identifying responses*, through feeding back initial responses and liaising with the provider as a preparation for a subsequent follow-up review with the responsible member of staff.
4. *Evaluating activities*, through assessing overall outcomes in conjunction with the provider against the original aims and objectives.

The importance of this type of approach is that it establishes a consistent procedure known to all staff and to the providers involved. It also ensures that any necessary steps are undertaken to obtain an effective and efficient activity which gives value for money. A significant and common anxiety for those negotiating CPD provision involves the need to identify and write success criteria. This is partly because 'it is not always possible to identify markers which can be assessed during the time required in the evaluation process'. Linked with this point, Whitcombe (1992) stresses the need to articulate clear objectives and relevant outcomes, and the need to use precise language in writing the CPD brief so that both targets and outcomes are fully understood by those involved.

The case study school in the example has invested a considerable amount of effort in developing negotiation skills and processes because it believes there is a significant pay-back for the school and (more pragmatically) because it can 'play the INSET market' since 'providers know that we're setting them the task of meeting our needs... and they also know that, with four university departments and two colleges of higher education as well as three lively LEAs, we can always go to alternative providers'. Clearly, this situation is unlikely to be the case for other schools. However, the ability to negotiate effectively remains pertinent to many in the new INSET environment.

As school managers gain experience in negotiating provision they are, to a greater or lesser degree, dependent on their own level of awareness and their need to match the type of CPD required with the known characteristics of providers and procedures to identify the best value for money. This has led to senior managers focusing more objectively on cost-benefit analysis in the selection of potential support agencies. One PDC argues, nevertheless, that making choices still remains difficult because 'the various providers can be grouped into the LEA, the university sector and private providers... but things are not that simple... because for example, they all provide distance-materials of some sort, they can all offer consultancy and they all run some kinds of courses'. A survey respondent also comments that 'there is a fourth providing group of increasing importance... the schools themselves... and we need to invest in training the trainers so that we can be more effective'.

Evaluating Providers

LEA Advisory, Inspection and Support Services

School responses to annual KEEP surveys provide evidence of the perceived advantages and disadvantages of each group of providers. Table 3.3 summarizes the most frequently mentioned comments from secondary schools in the 1995 survey. The same feature sometimes appears in both 'advantages' and 'disadvantages' columns, demonstrating the complexities involved in evaluating INSET provision.

Table 3.3 *Advantages and disadvantages of LEA provision 1995*
(54 responding secondary schools)

Advantages	Mentions	Disadvantages	Mentions
School is known to LEA	14	Limited school focus	9
LEA staff are known in school	16	Limited staff quality	7
Negotiated and responsive offer	17	Predictable offer	5
Local access and known venue	18	Service delivery problems	9
Network and shared view	12	Parochial, complacent	10
Good quality provision	8	Variable quality of provision	23
Based on local knowledge by LEA	8	Restricted response to need	6
Good value for money	14	Poor value for money	5
Administration easy	4	Administrative problems	3
		Tension over OFSTED link	7
		Anti-GM schools	3
Total advantages mentioned	111	*Total disadvantages mentioned*	87

Additional comments from a large number of secondary respondents showed that perceptions regarding advantages frequently turned on the convenience of 'the opportunity to negotiate local consultancies based on the staff which the LEA have available and our agreed needs', and 'the availability of locally tailored packages' offered by 'known and trusted staff who are known as part of the service'. Fuller explanations of disadvantages included the view that:

> the main income for the LEA advisory service now has to come from OFSTED preparation or inspection, and the need to get several advisers together to run a day course may conflict with these demands... as a result we are left feeling that we have to wait our turn.

This comment also underpins the view that 'we need to be able to plan well in advance... the local programme is offered termly and even that is under threat if the advisory staff are called away to other work'.

A major complaint is that 'the LEA is now running down... the good staff have gone into inspectorate work or moved into other areas of education, and the poor or complacent ones are left – not to respond to our needs but to offer what they think we want... those days are gone!' Although advantages usually outweigh noted disadvantages for various attributes, a number of schools question the variable quality of provision linked to staffing, either because the course failed to meet expectations, or where course content was poorly negotiated to meet school needs.

However, 1995 responses show a decline in INSET administrative problems with, on balance, schools still valuing and emphasizing LEA services. Nevertheless, adverse comments from GM schools still reflect an ideological rift with parent LEAs which 'is improving with the fullness of time, but which makes us feel that we are the outsiders although we pay the commercial rate for the services we buy'. Two PDCs also suggest that LEA packages which 'are of the "take the lot or leave it" type' are actually inhibiting school planning processes and efforts to meet their own needs, but another three suggest that the shift from LEA courses to LEA consultancy has been very much welcomed since it is more effective in supporting development needs.

Similar views are expressed by primary school staff. In a smaller sample – some 40 schools in 1995 – the same concerns are expressed about variable and declining quality attributable to the 'demands of OFSTED' which is 'taking the better trainers away for the [inspection] work and leaving us with the remaining staff who are usually of poorer quality and less able to respond flexibly to our needs... they continue to offer what we do not want'. Despite this, the advantages are still evident where LEAs have responded to schools' needs, since as one headteacher notes, 'they continue to recognize that they must be as good as the best if we are able to purchase where we will... and in doing this they are capitalizing on the closeness of geography and relationships'. The benefits of local financial arrangements are also recognized, but the evidence is that primary schools continue to purchase to meet needs which have been agreed with their LEA and which can be most readily met within a local situation – especially where 'the costs of supply staff and the need to pay for transport can be overcome if we use local provision for courses'.

In your experience…

In what ways have you found that your local LEA advisory service has changed its philosophy and practice in order to meet the needs of a changing environment? How far is your LEA concerned to actively 'market' itself?

You may feel that ties with your LEA have become more strained and distanced in some respects, particularly where it seems insufficient advisory staff are available to offer support. Alternatively, it may be that a shift to LEA agency status has led to closer ties between your particular LEA and local schools with, for example, the development of critical friend support for school-based developments. In some areas, traditional, centrally organized off-site courses are becoming school-based.

In others, LEAs have become aware of deficiencies in their profile and have begun to hire 'expert' consultants to represent them in specific areas of CPD, passing on costs to participating schools. From a school viewpoint, this may be more economic, alleviating the need to spend time negotiating services individually, and from an LEA viewpoint, they are able to meet school needs while matching more effectively the expertise and perceived strengths within HEIs and private consultancies.

Higher Education

Schools' use of higher education provision has been helped by school-focused and school-based developments in initial teacher training, which offer professional development opportunities for staff. One deputy head saw this 'as the only way forward in getting myself that additional training I needed… working with the college I also get the chance to be involved in a working party and we are now moving on to seek accreditation'. Table 3.4 summarizes perceived advantages and disadvantages of HEI provision and shows that the degree of match between comments is not as marked as for LEAs. This may suggest that HEIs need to make greater efforts to explain their potential value to 'client' schools and would benefit from marketing themselves more effectively. The smaller number of responses in the 1995 survey is also perhaps indicative of the limited use made of HEIs, 'partially because they are not known, and also because they are not good at selling what they have to offer'.

Table 3.4 *Advantages and disadvantages of HEI provision 1995*
(54 responding secondary schools)

Advantages	Mentions	Disadvantages	Mentions
Research base	5	Too remote from reality	4
Staff expertise	4	Staff 'out of touch'	6
Staff/ideas up-to-date	3		
Offer a different viewpoint	7		
Good quality overall	7	Variable quality	2
Negotiated offer	3	'Off the shelf' offer	3
Accreditation	6		
		Travel to centre/time lost	12
		Costs	9
School improvement focus	2		
Total advantages mentioned	37	*Total disadvantages mentioned*	36

HEIs have particular advantages in that they are able to offer schools the opportunities to participate in collaborative research alongside HEI staff , especially in relation to focused small-scale projects which fit with the school development plan. Disadvantages spring from 'the fact that we'd like to take advantage of what they've got to offer... but really... we can't... we're inhibited by the distance and the problems of getting them to respond to our particular needs at the point we need them'. In addition, problems arise from 'the lack of training that some of their staff have in delivering what's really very valuable material...' and 'some very useful ideas based on their research... what they've got to say is potentially very useful to us'.

Secondary schools were particularly concerned about continuing problems regarding accurate information about course content, course leaders, the need for evaluation and overall quality assurance issues. While adverse comments balance positive ones, when cost concerns are considered, quality indicators continue to favour HEIs over other providers.

By comparison with 1993 comments, for example, HEIs are seen by schools to have moved rapidly to meet earlier criticisms, to establish a market niche in school-based and negotiated consultancies where 'they offer more than the LEA can because they pull on staff from a wider range of specialisms', and have 'a greater willingness to respond to school needs'. While schools now appear more prepared to work with HEIs it is, nevertheless, on their own terms and in their own environment. Fifty of the 54 schools continue to work with the HEIs in initial teacher education, since it 'gives us a bargaining counter in working with the colleges because we manage to get the involvement of their staff as part of the equation in making facilities available for them'.

Current evidence indicates that the link between HEIs and primary schools has diminished over recent years. This may be because LEAs have endeavoured to nurture and maintain INSET provision for their primary schools, but the lack of HEI use is seen by one primary head as a 'result of providing us with what they think we ought to want when we have real needs which we seem not to be able to express', or because 'they are a long way away from us and we seem to exist in a different world where the daily demands of the school must come first'. The most frequent adverse comments concern the possible remoteness of university and college staff both geographically and from the world of the classroom, but there are also key comments about costs which are considered too high.

The HEI advantages most frequently highlighted by schools include access to current research knowledge. This is particularly valued at present because of the high profile gained by 'school improvement' and 'school effectiveness' research which has even proved influential at national government level with the establishment of a School Improvement Advisory Group set up by the Secretary of State in the Major government. Research is also valued by schools and individuals for the way it underpins courses, consultancy and networking (often facilitated through teacher training partnerships) which 'gives us the chance to meet people at the sharp end of research and to understand what's happening'. Another increasingly appreciated (though often undersold) HEI attribute is the offer of accreditation towards professional awards in, for example, mentoring, management, or specific curriculum expertise with possible credit accumulation and transfer facilities.

Accumulated evidence highlights several problems which HEI staff need to address in future in meeting primary schools' needs. One headteacher suggests that HEI agency provision, with complete service-level agreements, should be developed since disappointments over LEA provision and 'the demise of the teachers' centres has left us without a common local meeting ground where networks can develop'. HEI agencies may, however, be a problematic option, despite the fact that several universities have already developed OFSTED-related inspection agencies, usually headed by former HMI and staffed by early retired inspectors. The initial funding for HEI agencies, cost-effectiveness requirements and scale of operation may be too risky a financial and personnel commitment for HEIs at present and in any case, may not be viewed as part of their overall strategic mission.

Independent Agencies and Consultancies

Premature retirement opportunities resulting from post-1988 reorganization have created a pool of often active 'grey power' consultants and trainers with advisory backgrounds and particular expertise in education management, cross-curricular and subject specialisms. These consultants have been recruited through independent agencies offering courses, conferences and consultancies, or have become self-employed, developing their own networks of institutional contacts where critical friendship may be valued. However, schools often remain wary since 'we know the people who we used to work with, but we don't know anything of the quality of others in the field and there is some worry that they may be the people that former LEAs and colleges wanted to move along'.

Comments from those attending independent or private consultancy-run courses suggest they have two advantages: events are held in high quality environments and course leaders' presentational skills are often extremely good. Disadvantages spring from high costs and potential travelling distances. However, where independent consultancy support is used to develop school-based activities, they are often regarded as 'excellent in providing a slick and interesting presentation on topics of special expertise such as health and safety, but it is often "a package" on offer rather than a negotiated input which would best suit our needs'. LEA and HEI provision had, for one headteacher, the 'hidden advantage of a created network but independent providers bring diverse people together fleetingly'. That said, some respondents praised the often inspirational qualities of many independent consultants and valued the continuing and growing association they had with particular consultants.

Schools' use of independent services increased by 15 per cent between 1993 and 1994, but has fallen back in the 1995 sample, with PDCs suggesting that this is attributable to their comparatively high costs, to improvements in the quality of LEA and HEI consultancy and to the fact that some independent providers are now also heavily involved in OFSTED inspections. In short, as one deputy head argued, 'the market effect has led to a levelling up of quality from the LEA and HEI services and there is a continuing feeling that these are the services which we are drawn towards unless we need a very special expertise'.

Schools as Providers and Facilitators

The need for a variety of activities, as well as the demands involved in meeting individual, departmental and whole-school needs, has led to developing expertise within schools in managing and delivering school-based INSET. Inservice days are often used to allow departmental staff, year groups or other working parties to pursue particular themes and INSET days are often led by senior managers or other staff. The value of in-house group work was summed up in one interview where an HOD noted that:

> time for reflection and to discuss what we are doing and why we follow particular lines of development is at a premium and we gain so much from the mutual support amongst a group of people who know and generally trust each other.

In your experience...

What are the advantages of learning with, and from, your colleagues 'in-house'? What disadvantages have you found in working within your own organizational environment when undertaking professional development?

You may have identified a range of advantages – and disadvantages! – in working with colleagues on an in-house basis. While there are undoubtedly benefits in terms of greater professional cohesion, increased personal confidence and the opportunity to develop a better sense of institutional direction, there may also be problems. For example, an overly used or overly managed diet of site-based development can create a kind of 'false collegiality' which simply masks difficulties rather than addresses them and there are dangers that schools and individuals may begin to 'recycle inadequacies' rather than move beyond them.

Oldroyd and Hall (1991) discuss possible approaches to school-based INSET and also indicate the potential for problems, eg, where in-house staff trainers and presenters may not have sufficient expertise to develop confidence in colleagues; may have too narrow and introspective a focus; may overburden colleagues in terms of preparation and delivery; and may be seen to have their own private agenda which conflicts with group expectations.

Experience in one of the KEEP case study schools suggests that where 'in-house consultancy' is part of the culture of mutual sharing, support for colleague-presenters is strong and 'we gain from presenting the training because we want to demonstrate the very best to our colleagues'. The school's annual conference uses an external lead speaker to provide a structure for the various components, with three workshop sessions led by school staff offering linked contributions through demonstrations, discussion and materials development. Similarly, subject coordinators in one of the primary schools lead in-house activities in turn. They begin with 'a statement of rationale, approach and content, and then move on to demonstrations appropriate to each age group with the staff as class members'.

Reflection...

Are school or college-based development sessions a means of 'getting INSET on the cheap'? What are – or might be – the key benefits for your own organization from 'in-house' activities, particularly those undertaken during the past year?

Overall, in-house programmes may have the advantages of cheapness, collegiality and the chance to build on known relationships. Limitations often relate to content, may suffer from the 'familiarity breeds contempt' syndrome in terms of personnel, and sometimes 'fail to bring the newer ideas which may be imperative for effective change'.

Using a Range of Providers

PDCs generally attempt to avoid the negatives in school-based INSET by using a variety of professional providers as support. The *aide-mémoire* in Box 3.4 is based on the checklist used by one of the KEEP schools to determine each aspect of its CPD programme.

Box 3.4: Planning in-house professional development; an *aide-mémoire*

1. What aims do we have for the session(s)?
2. What kind of development strategies/methods do we want to use?
3. Which and how many staff are we catering for?
4. What is the learning context?
5. What environment and atmosphere do we want to create?
6. What level of 'trainer' input do we need?
7. Who could contribute from within the school?
8. Could any external providers usefully contribute? Who?
9. What are the various cost implications for the activity?
10. Does what we're planning fit into our overall professional development plan?
11. How does what we're planning contribute to the school's development plan?

In reviewing these considerations a school may choose to draw from a variety of providers using differing approaches at differing levels. For example, one member of staff argued that this kind of system had resulted in an over-use of cascade methods derived from external course attendance and follow-up departmental meetings, although another countered that selecting provision according to known criteria was generally more successful than using the system of guest speakers and departmental meetings which had been organized previously.

Experience in using multiple providers can be illustrated by reference to two international exemplars from North America and New Zealand. In both examples, schools are free to participate or not in a variety of initiatives, although the senior management team in each school is under an inherent local political pressure to take advantage of at least some of the opportunities offered. Schools can, however, select activities which they feel best meet specific needs. In particular, because INSET is funded by local school boards, the decision to participate is prompted by the quality of what is on offer without reference to cost considerations.

The examples chosen in Boxes 3.5 and 3.6 are both relatively well known and have been copied throughout North America and Oceania. The first, from North America, considers the use of a consortium approach in a group of Canadian schools where senior staff in schools, teacher training colleges, the local university and the teachers' union have planned joint activities at several operational levels.

Box 3.5: The Halton Effective Schools Project, Southern Ontario, Canada

Guiding principles:
  (a) School-based planning
  (b) Expertise to be developed in:
    – curriculum management;
    – classroom management; and
    – instructional skills and strategies

Participation: 43,000 students in 83 schools
Leadership: School board director of education and central task force of advisers and principals

Staff development: Through participation is some or all of the following, according to assessed need:

  (a) *Learning consortium* – schools linked to university for planned development work
  (b) *Summer institutes* – cooperative group learning at residentials on coaching and mentoring

---

(c) *Partners in the classroom* – training for paired mentoring, backed by development sessions

(d) *Leadership effectiveness* – focus on principals as instructional leaders

(e) *School growth planning* – five day inservice for senior school teams in management of change

(Stoll and Fink, 1988)

The second example, from New Zealand, is nationally funded and offered to meet the varying needs of the participating schools in a flexible way.

Box 3.6: New Zealand – Achieving Charter Curriculum Objectives

Guiding principles:
(a) Solid theoretical underpinning
(b) Collaborative decision-making
(c) In-school time for development and reflection
(d) Need for teachers to appreciate why help is of value

Participation: Six colleges of education, 50 schools

Leadership: Principals plus college staff as in-school consultants

Staff development: Through each school using a variety of approaches according to locally assessed need but all recognized the following qualities for effective school-based, externally supported help.

(a) *Participation* – need for communication and meeting skills

(b) *Extra resources* – need for time but also encouragement and consultancy support

(c) *Relevance* – in-school opportunities were a response to need, better than off-site courses

(d) *Variety of strategies* – importance of facilitators and networked exchange of ideas

(e) *Catalyst skills* – value of focus, keeping to plan, access to ideas and skills

(Rae, 1994)

Whereas the Halton opportunities are managed within a school board area, in New Zealand and the UK schools are largely autonomous managers of their own professional development with the decision to use particular strategies being an internal matter. Both the Halton and New Zealand schemes do, however, offer networking arrangements, which may be missing within the UK. One deputy head in a KEEP case study school asserted that 'there used to be a purpose in LEA meetings which went beyond course content, and the decline of the programme of meetings has now resulted in less contact... as a result we are looking to alternative links... in this we expect to gain more from the HEI'.

Amongst KEEP survey schools a variety of networks are being established which help to 'reduce the sense of isolation – especially if you're the only specialist teacher in the school', which 'allow for sharing and getting support in thinking over ideas... and sorting out what works'; and which provides 'an opportunity to pull back... to give me a chance to test ideas out with other colleagues'.

Managing the Information

The three main external providers of professional development – LEA, HEI and independent providers – generate and circulate a considerable amount of information . LEA materials are generally only circulated within their traditional area, although where schools are near authority borders marketing is now increasingly competitive. Similarly, HEIs generally circulate their own geographical areas, partnership schools and traditional areas of influence which have often grown from those areas served by the former Area Training Organizations. Independent providers tend to circulate information through contacts on either a limited local or national scale according to the agency size and function.

LEAs are most frequently criticized by PDCs for distributing INSET information too near events, effectively inhibiting longer-term school-based planning. HEI provision is often seen as irrelevant for subject staff in schools, and independent consultancies often send 'a glossy offer, but [it's] often from an unknown quantity who may or may not know the school'.

In your experience...

What criteria would you use in determining the potential usefulness of INSET publicity information? How far does the publicity you receive from LEAs, HEIs and independent consultants appear to match your criteria?

Your criteria may include attractiveness and presentation, detail and content, and the way in which information shows how the activity is targeted at the audience. You may be critical of various publicity materials because, for example, they

- lack clear statements regarding target groups and their existing level of expertise/experience;
- lack detail of providers' experience and expertise;
- lack any detailed description of delivery methods; and
- lack details of planning, structure and subsequent feedback evaluation options.

Schools may be aware of these features if, for example, they have already established an INSET database containing post-activity evaluations, which are used in subsequent CPD decision-making. For example, four of the 12 KEEP case study schools now use their own databank for all off-site activities. At its most complex, records include reviews of content, structure, delivery, relevance and overall effectiveness. Future requests can then be matched against computer records.

In addition, several project schools continue to rely on central LEA records. However, the 'system is suffering because the LEA lacks the administrative back up... schools are now slow to send in post-course information'. One headteacher argued that the most effective screening of activities took place through an insistence that every member of staff attending external events should report back at the next departmental or staff meeting: in this way, the reputation of presenters becomes established. In addition, both a deputy head and an HOD working with partner HEIs felt that post-course staffroom discussions were successful for 'spreading the word' and 'reviewing the benefits'.

Survey evidence shows that those managing CPD need to be aware of the importance of directing INSET information appropriately and speedily. Within the secondary sector, 60 per cent of survey schools delegate departmental and team activities to responsible staff – usually HODs. In a further 5 per cent of schools senior staff oversee planning, though many feel that opportunities to participate 'depend on the head of department – what's offered depends on their knowledge of potential help and awareness'. (The HOD's role is considered further in Chapter 5.)

In the primary sector, information tends to be discussed at staff meetings on a regular basis, or is normally directed by the headteacher according to perceived staff needs. By contrast, a number of secondary school teachers argued that 'the further down the line you are, the more likely it is that you'll have to take the initiative yourself. It seems that there is a continuum between those schools making considerable efforts to ensure that all opportunities are known, through to those who display activities but leave staff to find the material themselves; to those who ultimately leave everything except whole-school activities to the initiative of staff.

Our research shows that this last scenario appears to create general staff frustration because only dedicated and tenacious individuals prepared to seek out information tend to gain access to courses and activities. One headteacher openly acts as a 'screen', only passing on information on 'those topics and to those staff who have been identified as having particular needs in the development plan'. This approach occasionally occurs less overtly in other schools, where senior managers either attempt to protect staff from perceived 'professional overload', or wish to limit disruptions to school routines, or wish to prevent complex decision-making between competing requests.

While PDCs may raise staff interest by matching needs and highlighting opportunities, several teachers comment on the need for greater guidance on 'precisely what's permitted.... It's not always clear'. The checklist in Box 3.7, based on one used by a case study school, helps staff ensure that their CPD applications meet the criteria for support.

Box 3.7: Meeting the criteria for INSET opportunities

1. Try to obtain information on three possible sources   Please attach

2(a) For individual submissions: Please attach
List time needed, dates and costs, etc.

2(b) For working group, team or departmental submissions: list participants, time needed, dates, cost for each, etc.   Please attach

3. Have staffing implications been noted by
 – Head of department? (if appropriate); and   HOD?
 – Deputy head responsible for CPD?   DH?

4. Can provision be made internally?   Yes___ No___
Comment

5. In what way could the LEA meet requirements? (Course? Consultancy?)   Comment:

---

6. In what way could a local HEI assist?   Comment:

7. Could an independent course or consultant   Comment:
   help?

8. Recommendation and justification: what is   Comment:
   the preferred option and why?

9. DH (PDC) Comment.

Reflection...

How far might such a checklist be tailored and adapted to meet your own institution's needs? Are there any difficulties with using such a checklist?

The most frequent response tends to be that such procedures take up valuable time and may actually be of only limited value. Whatever system is used, it should only be introduced after a review of the specific cost-benefit equation appropriate to a particular institution's environment and its overall requirements.

Schools Managing the Market

When inservice education and training was controlled and managed though local authority advisory services, the degree of choice offered to schools was often limited by an LEA's particular strategic focus and concerns. Consequently, there was usually only limited scope for schools to utilize external providers without incurring considerable bureaucracy. Training and development opportunities were normally provided through LEA events subject to headteacher approval, with supply staff paid for centrally, as appropriate. The post-1988 movement away from what was often characterized as traditional LEA paternalism with its 'command and control' infrastructures towards the concept of the 'self-managing school' (Caldwell and Spinks, 1988) and the 'enabling LEA' meant that local authorities needed to come to terms with the fact that they were effectively faced with 'losing an empire and finding a role' (Audit Commission, 1989; Harland *et al.*, 1993). This shift in purchasing power and management responsibility has, however, led to simultaneous growth in administration within schools, with INSET contributing increasingly to the overall load.

Both the 1993 secondary and 1994 primary survey investigations brought frequent comments detailing the 'cumbersome' and 'almost impossible' administrative procedures required by LEAs, which arose from the need to claim costs for course attendance or to re-charge for advisory time so that no school within an LEA drew more than its fair proportion of LEA-allocated resources. A further drawback was that support for events and consultancy was determined by LEA advisory staff rather than school staff, 'often in an attempt to make the offer match the availability of staff at any one time'. During what became a transitional stage in PDC management, the only alternative for staff was limited opportunities for participation in one-term or one-year courses – often linked to HEIs and subject to the headteacher's support, the availability of LEA secondment opportunities and the availability of suitable provision. This option rapidly diminished almost immediately following changes to INSET funding.

Since schools have taken full management responsibility for determining their own CPD programmes, INSET has become much more market-focused and demand-led. For example, courses are now only run where they are clearly financially viable; secondments are rare; a variety of part-time and distance learning strategies are used to support professional development; and funding has become individualized rather than corporate. In addition, the language of the market has pervaded professional development, with 'providers' offering 'service-level contracts' and 'negotiating' to 'deliver' 'quality packages' to their 'clients'.

While the UK has led these changes, a number of European countries are also establishing demand-led INSET. For example, although INSET administration remains heavily centralized, Luxembourg now offers a range of courses according to national priorities with a guarantee that all those wishing to participate in any year will, if they have not used their 40 hours training allocation, be given opportunities to pursue activities of their choice. Ireland has established 25 teachers' centres capable of expanding to meet specific CPD demands and offering professional development programmes to meet both national and local needs, with participation on a voluntary basis. In Sweden, local authorities are organizing provision to meet needs identified within their area and based on an agreed proposal from the schools and the inspectorate. Financial control does, however, remain with the local education authority.

Despite these European trends, UK schools have both significantly greater management responsibilities and more opportunities to structure and prioritize their own developments. They are able to determine their CPD strategy in response to OFSTED action-planning obligations or according to internally determined preferences and priorities. The impact of professional development is likely to be influenced both by organizational circumstance and the nature of a school's INSET culture, with development profiles becoming increasingly institution-specific. One school may, for example, see an inspection-related issue as central to its development, while another may focus on an overarching whole-school issue like SEN; and yet another may decide to review teaching and learning skills through a departmental perspective. In view of these individual circumstances, an institutionally driven focus is more likely to impact on success than a situation where provision continues to be determined on a local authority-wide or nationwide basis bringing, perhaps inevitably, potential difficulties over 'ownership' and commitment.

CHAPTER 4

'Measuring' the Impact of INSET

Attempts to measure the impact of CPD are fraught with difficulties: evaluations have invariably been reliant on participants' self-reports and reviews (Bradley and Howard, 1992; Halpin *et al.*, 1990; Law and Glover, 1993; Triggs and Francis 1990). While the evaluation of training is a relatively longstanding practice, it remains notoriously problematic to capture an independent assessment of the impact of INSET on teachers' practice within classrooms. Efforts to measure the impact of teachers' CPD experiences on their students' learning present an even more complex set of problems.

Despite such challenges, some consideration of the impact of CPD on teaching and learning now contributes to school inspection assessments undertaken by OFSTED. Analysis of 100 of OFSTED's early inspection reports published since 1993 points to a number of key elements which inspectors regard as contributory factors in establishing school success and reflects some of the key qualities involved in managing resources. Links between specific comments made by inspectors regarding professional development and their more general comments within reports show that where effective planning is integral to a school's culture, its staffing resources are more likely to be maximized and used to advantage (Levacic and Glover, 1995).

Developing a Planned Approach

HMI (1993) note that 'involvement with staff development activities did not always result in changes of practice' and that this 'was frequently the result of poor management within the schools and the teachers' low expectations of their pupils rather than a reflection of the quality of the INSET'. The need for well-structured planning and management is also emphasized within OFSTED inspection reports. One report, for example, notes that where 'the staff development plan links staff training to faculty development plans...

83

there is a clear sense of direction and purpose in staff development planning and the priorities have been identified accurately'. OFSTED reports also stress that clear costings are essential in order to 'maintain a balance between priorities identified in the appraisal process, departmental priorities and whole-school priorities'. This is significant because in successful schools 'links have been made with the training needs of individuals, moving from a system where funds were allocated to departments to manage, to a system which links to whole-school priorities'.

Overall, OFSTED reports attempt to identify tangible connections between proposed professional development and IDPs so that resources effectively back up intentions. In one school, for example, the view was taken that the 'staff development programme is starting to focus more effectively on assisting teachers to meet the targets set in the school development plan'.

In your experience...

How is the link between your institution's development plan and professional development expressed and explained to you and your colleagues?

You may consider that your own institution has made only limited reference to the relationship between its development plan and professional development, perhaps because professional development issues, until recently, only attracted limited attention; because schools are still learning the art of integrating all aspects of their development planning and perhaps because communication networks within the institution are less effective than they might be. The increasing focus on strategies for school improvement and effectiveness combined with the introduction of OFSTED inspection has, however, brought a significant change in perspective.

While OFSTED inspectors comment on various aspects of planning and prioritization, detailed analysis of their reports shows that only 16 per cent of schools attract positive comments for the quality of their links between professional development and whole-school planning. A further 44 per cent are commended for specific aspects of their staff development, including appropriate systems, coherent planning, the integration of personal, departmental and whole-school targets, as well as PDCs' skills and breadth of view. The pressure for change is indicated by adverse comments made in almost a quarter of reports (24 per cent), where the need to link school development priorities with appropriate system development to encourage staff participation is most frequently mentioned.

As willing participants in the KEEP research study, case study schools are more likely than other schools to have reflected on their strengths and weaknesses in relation to CPD provision and organization. At the outset of the research all schools had PDCs and in-house consultative networks; 75 per cent said they had a staff development plan linked to school development priorities; and 85 per cent said they had consciously attempted to meet competing demands for individual, departmental and institutional development in a structured manner. Despite such positive indications of CPD commitment, it is important to recognize that the presence of structures and systems does not necessarily guarantee the effectiveness of provision.

The links between organizational structure and effective schooling have been implied in the rationale for development planning offered by Hargreaves and Hopkins (1991), who highlight the advantages for personal morale and self-esteem. While development planning may be an important motivator, it nevertheless remains true that the impetus towards development may be lost if, like all learning, the effectiveness of the process is not monitored and evaluated.

Monitoring the Process of Development

O'Sullivan *et al.* (1988) suggest that monitoring in CPD is 'a short term, immediate check on the delivery of staff development activities', while evaluation is 'a longer term judgement as to the worthwhileness of the staff development event, or a series of events'. In effect, monitoring is concerned with the ways in which intended plans are operationalized, while evaluation focuses on determining and assessing their impact. In reviewing training and development activities, Easterby-Smith (1986) asserts that evaluation has three purposes:

1. *proving*: demonstrating conclusively that something worthwhile has resulted from staff development;
2. *improving*: focusing on current and future programmes and trying to ensure that improvement occurs;
3. *learning*: recognizing that evaluation is 'an integral part of the learning and development process itself' since it cannot be separated off from the process on which it focuses.

OFSTED also stresses the importance of monitoring and evaluation as indicators that planning – rather than 'ad-hockery' – is being used to achieve stated aims. For example, one OFSTED school report comments that 'a monitoring system exists, but the inservice course evaluation forms provide little evidence of quality development'. By focusing on basic details in an effort to gain a high response rate from staff, the monitoring procedure for external activities used in one of the case study schools (see Box 4.1) may offer a possible starting point for examining the key elements required in developing effective monitoring processes.

Box 4.1: Monitoring procedure for external activities

1. Was the venue appropriate? Yes Fair No

2. Were the domestic arrangements satisfactory? Yes Fair No

3. General comments:

4. Did the activity:

   (a) achieve its objectives? Yes Partially No
   (b) stimulate? Yes Partially No
   (c) introduce new ideas? Yes Partially No

5. Were the content and presentation:

   (a) appropriate? Yes Partially No
   (b) lively? Yes Partially No
   (c) relevant? Yes Partially No

6. If this is a one-off activity, please indicate whether it:

   (a) has contributed to your personal development? Yes Partially No
   (b) has contributed to subject development? Yes Partially No
   (c) has contributed to the school development plan through cost effectiveness? Yes Partially No

7. Any other comments?

8. If this is a continuing activity notify DH of any problems immediately.

Reflection...

How does the monitoring procedure outlined compare with that which is used in your own institution? Where might improvements be made to current practice in your own organization?

There is no easy answer to this question. Effectively, each institution needs to establish its own 'bespoke' process and the parameters are an individual matter: the intention here is that your organization should use the above procedure as a starting point for critically evaluating its own practice!

Several questions in Box 4.1 relate to the quality of particular activities and reflect a concern to ensure that appropriate remedial action is taken where needed. However, monitoring may also need to focus fairly specifically on financial controls. For example, one headteacher comments that although monitoring 'is more time-consuming, it does ensure that we're seeing how much each activity costs... and how we need to use that sort of activity in future'. Nevertheless, several interviewees criticized financial control procedures which they saw as irritating and unnecessary, especially where 'we have to produce receipts for materials we've used which come from departmental stock and ought to be re-charged' or when 'we're often ending up out of pocket because, frankly, it's easier to get things ourselves than go through the whole purchasing procedure'.

Three case study schools suggest that monitoring enables their PDC to 'match our planned spending with the school's actual spending', so that departments 'are using delegated funds as intended', and that allocated funds are used in ways that 'seem real for staff'. Two interviewees also suggest that more open controls are a better means of ensuring that professional development gets its agreed funding allocation. In the only case study school where development funding was used to support all activities until funds ran out, there was a feeling that monitoring enabled 'a fairer distribution in the latter part of the year when there might be competition for what is available'.

In your experience...

How far does financial monitoring in your own school or college attempt to ensure that intentions match reality?

Your response may involve three levels of control: the use of funds to support the intended activities; the proper use of allocated funds; and the effort to achieve value for money. You may also feel that more open publication of running totals would assist in the process of resource management.

Survey data show that even well-structured school plans and priorities may be subject to change and unforeseen influences during the year which inhibit the possibility of earlier decisions being carried through in full. The need for contingency planning is increasingly emphasized by respondents in order to match changing circumstances. For example, in 1993, only 8 per cent of the survey schools said that they were likely to vire funds if problems arose during the year, with a common response being that 'while we're able to vire, we wouldn't do so because our funds are already minimal for our professional development needs'. By 1995, however, while spending is somewhat constrained within SPG (D) funds for GM schools and GEST funding for maintained schools, 45 per cent of secondary schools said they had vired funds; 58 per cent of these said they had done so in order to maintain teaching staff numbers, while 40 per cent of them had also used the vired funds to provide and maintain teaching resources.

Two interviewees also suggest that some 'hidden virement' may exist. Where for example, one school with an SPG (D) grant in excess of £50,000 only appeared to use £20,000 for professional development, the annual statement nevertheless was reconciled with the stated sum. This was through financial classification of 'resource purchases' by departments as 'curriculum development materials'. Although senior managers are actually only viring funds in ways they feel are justified as an extension of professional development, they are also aware of the need to maintain staffing levels so that 'if necessary all but the essentials of putting teachers in front of children will have to go'.

Our research also indicates that virement is more likely to occur in LEAs where the greatest level of underfunding exists: this is often a feature of rural areas. Moreover, lower levels of funding and more centralized administrative structures tend to characterize primary schools' CPD provision, limiting their opportunities to vire. While 24 per cent of primary schools say they could vire funds if they wished to, only 6 per cent of primary headteachers and PDCs say that they would actually do so. However, primary headteachers remain fearful that if funding pressures continue, they will be increasingly tempted to 'use funds for our basic job and replace any development or training with in-house activities so that we can keep within the law'. Clearly, if this happens the impact of development funding will be substantially minimized.

Evaluating for Effectiveness

Whatever the level or nature of funding, the impact of CPD on teaching and learning needs to be evaluated effectively in order to facilitate future planning. OFSTED reports suggest that evaluation should ensure that senior managers monitor and understand the work of staff as fully as possible, using line management or mentoring links, so that formal opportunities exist for appreciating both costs and benefits. OFSTED also notes the importance of involving governing bodies fully in the process so that they are aware of the potential and actual benefits arising from supporting INSET. It is stressed that evaluation should pick out both whole-school successes deriving from the school development plan and individual appraisal-related achievements. Known and publicized 'in-house' successes can enhance current development plans and impact on the kinds of teaching and learning strategies adopted.

OFSTED reports also point to the importance of organizational structures and evaluation processes on professional development. While 16 per cent of sampled reports recommend that management structures for professional development should be reviewed, inspectors also commend those schools which produce clear statements of staff entitlement to professional development opportunities, especially where these relate to an undertaking to meet appraisal-identified needs. The fundamental need for an effective appraisal system as a basis for personal professional development also attracts comment. For example, 56 per cent of reports commend appraisal practices, while 24 per cent suggest that some improvement in either appraisal-related structures or organization is advisable. Eighteen per cent of reports are critical of some aspect of appraisal practices within the school, especially where the targets are not used to underpin future planning.

OFSTED inspectors also stress the importance of involving staff fully in training and development programmes. In one school, inspectors point out that 'the deployment and development of all administrative staff is not formally monitored, and this should be reviewed', and in a number of others, inspectors make clear that for INSET to be effective, it needs appropriate personnel, materials and equipment support: for example, one report stresses that fundamental skills development in information technology is a priority training need for all staff in the school.

Where institutions have developed even embryonic evaluation processes, there is evidence of a considerable improvement in the quality of professional development provision. However, a key problem confronts many schools: the time used for evaluation detracts from that needed to implement changes or may overburden staff with 'yet another task'. Although most case study schools operate evaluation systems for their whole-school activities, with staff being asked to complete evaluation sheets following inservice days, there is little evidence showing how evaluation sheets are analysed or readily used to inform subsequent planning. There are, nevertheless, signs of progress. For example, in two schools the data compiled following their annual conferences are used to assess how far various school development targets appear to have been met through planned professional development during the year. This review forms the basis for future planning.

However, there are also costs. PDCs point to the 'considerable amount of effort which goes into maintaining a register of activities' including evaluation details, but recognize that 'this is really monitoring... and we don't do much to see what impact INSET is having on what we're doing in, say, six months time... we're really amateurs in that!'. However, in spite of the effort required, schools feel that appropriate and workable evaluation techniques make a key contribution to more effective management, even if the development process is a complex and time-consuming one. In one primary school with seven staff, a compromise has been reached with an annual review of CPD undertaken at a staff meeting. The costs and benefits of activities are discussed and then implications for future planning are fed into the development planning process.

Within a European context, monitoring and evaluation processes are also at an early stage of development (see Box 4.2). The pattern of involvement in CPD is generally more individualistic within mainland Europe: attendance is frequently voluntary and self-determined, and although evaluation sheets are used, they often focus on quality maintenance, with the impact of CPD on schools not being actively measured unless senior managers decide to maintain personalized assessment records for staff. By and large, however, the evaluation is designed to inform providers rather than provide either personal or group views of value to the schools or purchasers involved.

Box 4.2: Quality assessment, monitoring and evaluation in Europe

Italy

Assessment is the responsibility of those promoting inservice courses: they are required to assess participants' pre-course state of knowledge, the impact of the course, and the effect of this on teachers' cultural and professional development. The results of this assessment are transmitted to both local and national administrators who then submit plans for the following year based on identified continuing needs.

The Netherlands
Schools undertake their own inservice quality assessments for CPD they have purchased. Although this is supervised by the local inspectorate and training programmes must be submitted, neither standard plans nor formal evaluations are required.

Iceland
Following course participation, all participants are asked to complete a report on its usefulness and quality. Although these are used by providing agencies for their own evaluation, they are not part of school development assessment processes.

Reflection...

How far do you think evaluation practices in the UK are effective and at a higher level than that which appears to take place in these other European countries?

The essential difference between evaluation practices in England and Wales (and to a lesser extent those in Scotland and Northern Ireland), and those operating within many other European countries is that within the UK, professional development spending contributes to their annual budget and is controlled and managed by schools themselves rather than being administered by national or local agencies. Understandably, perhaps, British schools are more likely to be concerned with ensuring that they obtain value for money, with the perception often being that its 'school money we're spending'. KEEP survey evidence shows that this perception is contributing to the development of more systematic approaches to managing professional development.

Achieving Value for Money

While value for money concerns have already been mentioned in relation to institutional planning (see Chapter 3), survey evidence over several years also shows that PDCs are becoming increasingly expert at cost-benefit analysis when planning and evaluating CPD. Although they feel they are only 'working at a basic level to try to estimate value for money' they are not only interested in 'taking a bottom-line approach' but also make 'some decisions on our own hunch about what's likely to be good and what might be bad'. As a result, many feel much better placed to assess how far providers offer value for money, which they regard as an important piece of marketing information.

McMichael *et al.* (1995) examine the gains and losses resulting from secondment. Their research, which involved the Scottish Education Department, curriculum consultative groups and local authorities, based its analysis on assessing the gains and losses to secondee, seconder and receiving organization on appointment, in post and at exit. Strengths were seen to be gains in knowledge of management and organization, knowledge of the wider system, networking and increased contacts, independence, project development, and increased knowledge of theory and clarity of thinking. Costs to individuals involved personal disruption; while costs to employers involved loss of contact and the need to resettle returning secondees, and costs to the secondment institution involved managing activities and individuals on a short-term contract basis. Gaining value for money from the experience involved increasing the benefits for participants while reducing costs. However, it may be that costs and benefits are only measurable in general terms, apart from the opportunity to accredit experiential learning which allows the benefits to be translated into a 'professional currency', eg, a degree or diploma.

Value-for-money demands from schools – and especially from primary schools with more limited funds – have led to a more flexible pricing process. Many LEA agencies have developed a greater responsiveness to institutional needs by being prepared to negotiate, by demonstrating greater awareness of criticisms of former LEA provision and by attempting to rival private consultancy offers and professional practice (Law and Glover, 1996). In addition, headteachers consider that agency developments have enabled them to obtain better value for money because they feel they now have greater control over negotiations and are better able to determine the programmes offered. The external pressures which increase and enhance 'client power' are illustrated by the responsiveness of schools to the changing system. During 1995, secondary schools also claimed to be developing a greater awareness of value-for-money issues, partly because 'we can now purchase from a wider range but with declining funds we need to get the best possible deals... in that sense we're learning from the GM schools – although OFSTED has also taught us to be more careful'.

This raised awareness also relates to what staff take into account when they evaluate the 'balance between time out and the value gained compared with what the pupils might have lost'. While many acknowledge the problems of generalizing, a significant number of INSET managers are clear that LEAs offer the best value for money. Table 4.1 summarizes the secondary findings overall.

Table 4.1 *Assessing value for money (VFM) amongst alternative providers, secondary schools (numbers of responses for each provider)*

Ranking as VFM	LEA advisory	LEA courses	LEA consultancy	HE courses	HE consultancy	Private consultancy
1 (low)	4	4	1	4	1	5
2	8	8	6	4	2	4
3	14	12	10	8	2	1
4	7	13	13	4	4	7
5 (high)	6	7	5	4	3	7
Total mentions	39	44	35	24	12	24

In addition to their responses in Table 4.1, CPD managers were also asked to focus on their own personal training needs. The most frequent request from PDCs is for 'guidance on what is meant by, and how we secure, value for money', although it is essential not to evaluate this comment too narrowly as meaning that they lack confidence in their ability to buy in services. The PDC in one school, for example, rated all provision used recently at the highest level while asserting that 'we are now able to target for our need and to purchase the service which meets our specifications'.

Several PDCs asserted that 'we need to learn much more about the way we can negotiate for what we know are the school's needs... without providers telling us what they think we need', and also argued for better technical support. Furthermore, one PDC claimed that software for 'tracking all INSET participants and a database of information on quality and effectiveness so that we can reduce our administrative load' would be a valuable aid, while another thought that 'the value of what's being offered is much more enhanced if it's seen to contribute somehow to some form of individual accreditation'.

Gaining Credit for Achievement

Although staff perceptions of INSET are the focus of Chapter 5, professional aspirations are a crucial element in any evaluation of voluntary professional development. Interviewees tended to differentiate between what they saw as different kinds of INSET, identifying between professional development which has:

- a *contractual focus*, ie, is required as part of their conditions of service;
- an *institutional focus*, ie, is undertaken as part of general school development and support processes; and

- *a personal focus*, ie, is undertaken for personal professional development reasons.

While interviewees felt that combining all three aspects could be potentially difficult – especially since, in their view, 'sponsored' INSET nowadays often seems to be instrumental and contractually focused – several argued for the need to find ways of maximizing and integrating the benefits of all three elements, for 'your job, the kids and yourself'. Being able to do so increased professional motivation. One aspiring headteacher, for example, spoke of 'the need to do extra training, even if it's at your own expense, so that you develop the skills and competences which heads need'.

In your experience...

Try to review your professional development experiences during a specific period (eg, a term) and try to classify them under the following headings: (a) contractual; (b) institutional (c) personal professional. What might the results show about your own and your institution's approach to CPD? In particular, what motivated you to undertake any voluntary activities?

The motivators mentioned most frequently by staff in the case study schools are those connected with the sense of personal and institutional commitment, ie, becoming more effective practitioners and classroom teachers – as well as a perceived need to prepare oneself for future promotion. None of the survey respondents mentioned the possibility of gaining salary increases as a direct result of further training and development, though the sense of achieving more status was implicit in some comments. Accreditation as a recognition of voluntary commitment appears to be of considerable importance to a number of individuals because 'while we're prepared to pay for ourselves if necessary, we also need to have something to show for it'. In this respect, HEIs have significant advantages as providers who can link activities with accreditation through part-time certificate, diploma or degree courses.

Accompanying the decline in secondment opportunities and the concomitant decline in sponsored funding for long courses, there has been a growth in distance-learning opportunities. This development has helped to ensure that HEIs remain responsive to practitioner and 'client' demands for part-time learning opportunities. For example, one headteacher stressed that he 'would recognize the strength of those who present a degree gained by part-time and distance learning', although another argued that 'distance learning puts such pressure on the participant because he or she generally lacks the support which is usually available in traditional courses… when the going gets tough it's easy to say you've had enough'.

While accreditation for formal study is both valued and increasingly expected of individuals seeking promotion to senior management posts, there is also an institutional imperative towards accrediting professional development. Two-thirds of the Keele case study schools have established some form of accreditation linked with, for example, their LEA through joint work with a local HEI, or through course completion certificates which may give some credit for activities provided by recognized independent providers.

Access to information technology and computerized record-keeping developments are also supporting teachers' efforts to build CPD 'portfolios' linked to their professional experiences. Two case study schools provide their own certification for recognized 'in-house' activities undertaken as part of the school's CPD programme, while five also maintain profiles or records of training and development. Such evidence is then 'available when we go for promotion within the school, but they're also of interest to other schools when someone applies for a new post'.

Following on from the development of Records of Achievement for pupils, and profiles for trainee teachers, the concept of INSET portfolios and professional development profiles have increasingly become the concern of the government, which recommends 'profiles of competence which set out their [teachers] professional capabilities and give a picture of relative strengths and weaknesses' (DfE, 1993), as well as the TTA and education professionals themselves. While the issue of profiling remains contentious, with anxieties in some quarters over its potential use within a managerialist framework, the implications of profiling on professional careers remains as yet unclear. Nevertheless, practising teachers may find it useful to establish their own professional record of achievement as a more systematic record of professional strengths (Bolam, 1993; Earley, 1995; Law and Glover, 1995).

Profile development might be facilitated through, for example, the kind of Professional Development Record Sheet used in one case study school and kept in personal staff files for reference (see Box 4.3).

Our research shows increasing evidence that initial teacher training and professional development 'partnerships' between schools and HEIs are enabling the development of more flexible, modular programmes, particularly where thematic and reflective topics support school-based action research opportunities. In addition, parallel moves towards recognition and 'accreditation' at a whole-institutional level are occurring, with some of the earliest developments being based on the adoption of ISO 9000 (formerly British Standard 5750) by schools and colleges. West-Burnham (1992) details the

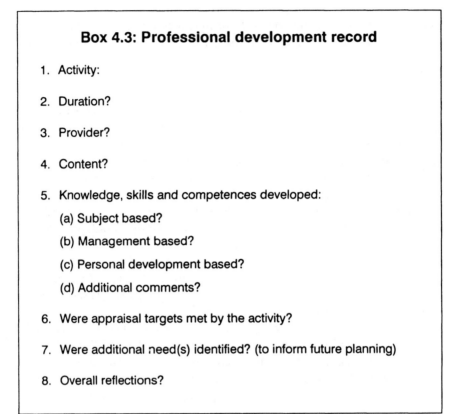

Box 4.3: Professional development record

1. Activity:

2. Duration?

3. Provider?

4. Content?

5. Knowledge, skills and competences developed:

   (a) Subject based?

   (b) Management based?

   (c) Personal development based?

   (d) Additional comments?

6. Were appraisal targets met by the activity?

7. Were additional need(s) identified? (to inform future planning)

8. Overall reflections?

process and also stresses that it is a means to developing quality systems rather than being a measure of quality itself. That said, schools using ISO 9000 have sometimes used it as a catalyst for identifying potential development structures to match the evolution of more effective management structures.

Organizational recognition for those achieving the Investors in People (IIP) standard has also been used by schools as a way of enhancing their institutional culture, so that professional development is subsumed within a human resource management framework built on shared values, effective leadership and team development. Both ISO 9000 and Investors in People schemes have positioned schools and colleges alongside other service organizations and industry.

Total Quality Management concepts are also being utilized in some schools with the aim of harnessing shared values amongst staff in order to pursue the goal of 'customer' satisfaction. This represents a cultural shift away from control or deficiency models of management towards an empowerment model which is based around organizational excellence. Training and teamwork are regarded as fundamental to this development (Oakland, 1989; Sallis, 1992) and development aims to help staff 'work smarter' as well as towards targets or 'outrageous goals' as a spur to organizational change and achievement (Murgatroyd and Morgan, 1992).

Reflection...

Walker and Scott (1993) have investigated the relationship between headteachers and senior management teams in a sample of ten Australian schools. Amongst their conclusions they refer to the following:

- *external matters were given only limited attention [by teams];*
- *principals appeared unclear about why they retained some matters for themselves;*
- *the rhetoric of openness needs to be transposed into reality;*
- *the way in which the school supports team membership and performance; and*
- *there is a case for identifying deficiencies in the team's operation and implementing strategies to rectify them (pp.38–9).*

What strategies associated with quality improvement might be applicable in a school where the senior management team feels that it may be underrated?

Your responses may be related to the use of systems which encourage open discussion and clear lines of responsibility and accountability. However, you may feel that while strategies may be suggested, success is dependent on recognition of the need to change and a willingness to change the organizational culture overall. The motivation for fundamental change depends on encouraging all stakeholders.

A collective imperative for school improvement may come through the external recognition of achievement. Some schools have participated in the Schools Curriculum Award, which evaluates the school within its community and which, in the words of one headteacher, is 'a means of keeping the focus on the school as a learning community compared with the stress which other schemes place on systems'. School staff who have won this or similar awards suggest that collective accreditation can, in appropriate circumstances, be very motivational, but as respondents in one school comment, it can sometimes be the case that 'the kudos rests rather more with senior management than with us as a staff' so that the longer-term effects of gaining one-off awards may, in reality, be rather limited.

Indeed, staff interviewees in three case study schools argue that a feeling of 'collective motivation' is not necessarily enhanced by such accreditation. It may instead be related to an overall organizational culture which has a clear development focus, rather than any attempt to enhance staff self-esteem through accrediting their work. One deputy head interviewee suggests that 'the marketing strength of accreditation might be greater than its effect on staff'. In fact, while most interviewees acknowledged that personal professional development is important to them, 'the real gain is in what we're able to do for youngsters in the classroom'.

Teaching, Learning and Institutional Improvement

Fisher *et al.* (1995) outline factors which match student perceptions of the classroom climate to similarly rated teacher perceptions of school climate. In doing so, they provide some evidence of common values within the schools they investigated: in a study of 48 Tasmanian schools they identified a link between teachers' views of a positive innovatory climate and students' views of their involvement in challenging classroom activities. The link was particularly marked in primary schools, where change appears to be more of a shared experience between teachers and taught, and then contributes to overall school effectiveness.

Eighty per cent of the primary and secondary schools surveyed during our 1995 research mentioned 'teaching and learning improvements' as a key institutional objective. Many also imply or suggest that professional development can have an important impact on teaching and learning quality. During periods of major national change, eg, the implementation of GCSE, and the National Curriculum, INSET had clearly defined objectives: to transmit information, to develop competence in new procedures, and to provide opportunities for skills development and practice.

In the case of National Curriculum implementation and insofar as subsequent teaching and learning is assessed through Key Stage pupil performance tests, a fairly clear relationship can be seen between government-driven training and outcomes. However, other factors are also important in identifying teaching and learning quality overall, like the extent to which a 'learning culture' exists within classrooms, the degree of change demanded of departments or individuals, and the resource base which facilitates change. In this respect, a reliance on the assessment of pupil achievement has very limited value in measuring INSET effectiveness.

Nevertheless, identifying success criteria – particularly within an action research project – may be helpful to school staff in evaluating the impact on specific aspects of teachers' practice. A good deal of action research involves teachers in individual or corporate planning for curriculum change, behavioural modification and educational processes, any or all of which may eventually lead to changes in classrooms which are measurable to some degree. For example, staff in one of the survey schools had noted a high and increasing incidence of verbal bullying amongst 12–13-year-old girls, leading to considerable unhappiness. Pastoral and curriculum committees were asked to suggest improvement strategies, which eventually led to several agreed recommendations (see Box 4.4).

Box 4.4: A possible improvement strategy

Joint Pastoral and Curriculum Working Group
Recommendations: Verbal bullying in Yrs 8 and 9

1. There appears to be a need for the problem to be 'worked through' since pupils feel that there is too much hidden unhappiness. The process needs to be identified and acted upon during the next term. We suggest efforts should be directed through the following *strategies*:

   (a) the pastoral and social education programme;
   (b) the drama programme;
   (c) parental awareness programme.

2. *Professional development needs* include:

   (a) time allocations for curriculum planning;
   (b) consultant input to foster both the curriculum planning and the management of behaviour groups;
   (c) a 'bullying'/behaviour speaker for the parents' evening.

3. *Success criteria* include:

   (a) a decline in the number of reported disagreements in Yrs 8 and 9;
   (b) increases in positive comments in the annual student survey;
   (c) improvements in attendance for targeted pupils (ie, those believed to have suffered);
   (d) improvements in tutor-assessed pupil self-esteem.

The school carried through the working group's recommendations and saw a considerable reduction in tension, not only because of improved relationships between pupils, but also because of raised pupil self-esteem and higher attendance rates. Measurable gains were noted. At an end-of-year evaluation session for staff, changes in pupil attitudes and staff expectations were acknowledged as real benefits. These were largely attributed to:

- raised awareness of behaviour problems amongst staff and pupils;
- increased levels of staff participation (up by over half) through pastoral programme changes;
- more open discussion of behaviour problems generally and the issue in particular between pupils;
- open discussion of the issue between pupils and staff;
- open discussion of the issue between staff.

While it was accepted that none of these changes was directly measurable, the impact of professional development – consisting of one focused staff meeting, 15 hours of group planning meetings, a parents' evening, and nine hours of advisory input – was recognized as being considerable.

A major effect of identifying potential change needs in an institution is that the resulting development strategies are likely to be seen as genuinely responsive rather than 'manufactured'. In this sense, the open acknowledgement that a problem exists facilitates the establishment of a 'shared development climate' which may then help bring about a resolution. In support of this, our annual survey evidence has identified increased efforts by both teachers and senior management to focus on organizational costs and benefits rather than to concentrate on individual gains or drawbacks in any development strategy. This was not a blind focus, however, While developing a whole-school perspective has the potential for much improved and integrated professional development leading to institutional success, teachers also noted that an overwhelming focus on organizational benefits can present negative outcomes: an apparent threat to the personal professional development of individuals, especially where personal needs do not immediately coincide with – or may even contradict – institutional priorities (Maclure, 1989).

Reflection...

How far have the development opportunities which your school or college has funded for you, actually benefited your own personal development plan as well as supported your professional role? Can both needs be satisfied simultaneously?

CHAPTER 5

Meeting Challenges, Making Responses

A Polarization of Perceptions

Recent studies indicate that teachers usually value CPD – both for the support it offers them as individuals and for the way it contributes to institutional and student success (Earley, 1995; Law and Glover, 1995). There are, nevertheless, significant variations in the degree to which CPD is perceived as beneficial. INSET is most positively regarded when it has been systematic, well-organized and builds on existing expertise. In such circumstances, teachers comment that it has been 'stimulating, boosted self-confidence and had a significant impact on their personal teaching methods' (HMI, 1993).

A minority of teachers are, however, less complimentary, pointing to flaws in both CPD provision and impact (Page and Fisher-Jones, 1995). In their evaluation of LEA-managed GEST, HMI note that 'a minority [of teachers] saw much of their LEA INSET experience as tangential to their purposes, or of limited quality, being poorly differentiated for individual need and lacking intellectual challenge' (HMI, 1993, para.21). Similarly, Earley's study (1995) found that 'poorly managed professional development activities tended to create a powerful antipathy towards training as a whole', while the TTA survey (Page and Fisher-Jones, 1995) found that 18 per cent of teachers felt CPD was limited in its impact on their classroom practice.

This apparent 'polarization of perceptions' is borne out by our research findings, which showed wide variations in the value which teachers and managers placed on their CPD experiences. While it was 'useful', 'beneficial' or 'valuable' for most people, the diversity of attitude reflects not only differences in personal experience, but also difficulties in measuring the impact and identifying the quality of CPD, whether individually, institutionally or nationally. For example, almost all our interviewees agreed that CPD has, at times, only a limited impact on classroom practice. Despite this, our survey confirms the TTA's results that CPD can be a very a positive experience, but one which should be more effective.

Aside from concerns over the quality and impact of INSET, interviewees were anxious that a developing accountability focus could jeopardize the voluntaristic tradition of INSET, leaving a more 'remedial' emphasis on 'correcting' bad practice. They were concerned that this focus could overemphasize a notion of 'compulsory CPD' to meet school-led targets, which may not be relevant or appropriate for individual needs as well. This was seen as potentially damaging to teachers' commitment.

Interviewees' questionnaire returns are also indicative of the complexity of viewpoint over the matter of compulsion. While 93 per cent considered that CPD 'should be an entitlement for all teachers', 57 per cent also agreed or strongly agreed that CPD 'should be compulsory: teachers and managers should have to undertake CPD regularly to maintain their registration as teachers and professionals'. Additional comments appear to indicate that, while many are unhappy over 'compulsion' focused on institutional needs, many see an 'obligation' to maintain personal professionalism as appropriate – 'doing a good job and being seen to do it'. Poorly handled 'obligatory' CPD, targeted at institutional needs and not on their own, was seen as counter-productive, demoralizing and demotivating to the teacher workforce.

The INSET Legacy

Teacher expectations are frequently influenced by their previous CPD experiences and the kind of professional culture within which they work. Long-standing and widely differing INSET traditions amongst LEAs have also encouraged assumptions about INSET entitlement and the value of CPD. Some LEAs, for example, were seen as highly paternalistic and protective, effectively 'spoon-feeding' schools within dependency cultures. Others appeared complacent by comparison – 'our LEA's always had a bit of a fat-cat syndrome' – sometimes neglecting or minimizing INSET opportunities and undervaluing potential. Yet other LEAs gained reputations as 'INSET havens' fostering highly innovatory development cultures, individual initiative, secondment opportunities and enhanced development roles in schools, sometimes at the risk of overspending the CPD budget! Despite the fact that schools now largely determine their own internal INSET strategies, these legacies remain influential within a number of school-LEA relationships, most obviously, perhaps, in relation to the primary sector (Law and Glover, 1995).

In your experience...

Are the legacies of previous LEA-school relationships still evident in the way your own institution works with local providers? How would you describe the INSET tradition which operates in your own school or college – could it be described as 'paternalistic', 'complacent' or 'innovative' in approach?

If your institution fits very obviously into one of the above somewhat stereo-typical categories, you may like to consider how far the tradition is being maintained within the new 'INSET marketplace'. Is it because it is beneficial to schools and colleges themselves or because 'that's the way it's always been'? Are institutions themselves being complacent about the relationship? Alter-natively, your school or college's relationships may differ from those outlined above (in which case how might it be characterized?).

An understanding of INSET traditions and legacies – what Earley (1995) calls their 'historical baggage' – is potentially valuable in evaluating changes to professional development practices and perceptions resulting from the priva-tization of INSET (Harland *et al.*, 1993). This, in turn, contributes to our understanding of the ways CPD impacts on teacher motivation, pupil achieve-ment and the development of institutional excellence.

This chapter examines teachers' perceptions of INSET, by considering how far teachers and managers perceive that CPD impacts on their personal and professional confidence, their classroom practice and their career aspira-tions. It also considers briefly whether teachers and managers perceive that differences exist in the ways different departments value CPD; how far gender influences attitudes to INSET; and whether seniority and organizational role are influential in determining the approach taken. Finally, it considers the institutional costs and benefits arising from CPD.

While the vast majority of school staff see CPD as personally and profes-sionally valuable, a minority feel it to be 'over-valued' or 'rather a drain on my time when there's so much teaching to do', particularly in respect of short courses and one-off events. Survey information also showed that, at one extreme, a small minority of headteachers and PDCs are somewhat disdainful of professional development, viewing the obligation to use professional de-velopment days as a 'necessary evil', which they felt were best used to catch up with National Curriculum work and related tasks (Glover and Law, 1995). In such schools, any professional development focus often gets subsumed by 'survival' concerns and exacerbated by unclear development policies and strategies. At the other extreme, a significant proportion of staff in project schools feel that CPD is becoming less marginal and more integral to institutional processes. Several argue it has the potential to provide highly valued and multi-faceted improvement opportunities, ideally enabling group and individual agendas to be combined within a whole-school focus, especially where the process is well structured and well managed.

KEEP survey evidence indicates that schools increasingly regard as insufficient the post-1988 'training' focus where knowledge and skills acquisition was emphasized. While the training focus still predominates, many are also now adopting broader development perspectives requiring longer-term strategies. While government and TTA publications tend to use the language of training at the level of specifics and the language of development in relation to generalities, a number of (often more senior) school staff appear inclined towards the more broadly based development emphasis – 'the ability to look at wider horizons' (primary headteacher) and the fact that it offers 'more opportunity for us to use time to reflect on what we're doing in the classroom' (secondary teacher).

Perceptions of Professional Practice

Both main scale and promoted staff recognize there are difficulties in trying to identify how INSET impacts on classroom and professional practices. Some interviewees feel constrained by a 'professional climate of more and more accountability' which 'drains your enthusiasm' and makes people feel increasingly pressurized to show how CPD improves teaching *and* stimulates student achievement.

The need 'to show its benefits straight away... when its not always like that' emphasizes the difficulties in trying to link CPD with day-to-day 'evidence' of outcomes in classrooms. The TTA survey comments that 'different people have different ideas as to the purpose of CPD', adding that 'if one assumes that it is primarily about improving the quality of teaching, CPD will have to change'. This concern that INSET should relate more closely to 'measurable' outcomes like improved classroom competences highlights the notorious difficulties faced by those evaluating professional development.

Although a majority of interviewees feel that 'pupils are benefiting from the investment of our time and money', they are also frustrated at the apparent stress laid on 'measuring everything – through league tables and lists'. A number of senior managers argue, for example, that the impact of CPD on teaching and management skills is 'unquantifiable', that it achieves 'something which can't always be shown', and that the benefits 'often only show up much later in your career'. One deputy head/PDC comments that:

I was very fortunate to work with a head who believed in giving people the chance to try things out and change roles – and by supporting us with various kinds of INSET... in some ways, it was a nuisance at the time... but the flexibility it gave me and my colleagues has... it's really paid off in the long term. I've got a lot from it professionally, but at the time I wasn't so sure.

In addition, one young teacher suggests that CPD which is 'really pinned down', where 'you have to show how everything's improving your teaching' will probably create increased anxiety and a sense that 'all the "aggro" won't be worth it... people just won't put themselves forward for training'.

In your experience...

Is INSET targeted at individual staff, departments and the institution where you work? How far is it legitimate to categorize people as CPD 'volunteers', 'conscripts' or 'conscientious objectors'?

You are likely to have found that opinions differ widely on the role of INSET and its potential use in institutional and personal development. It may be that you found particular attitudes characterize different departments or subject areas, or that younger members of staff display a different view of CPD from older or more senior colleagues, perhaps because experiences have changed assumptions and expectations over recent years. Some members of staff, particularly younger ones, may feel 'entitled' to support and development opportunities, while others may see it as an 'offer they can't refuse' but would like to – a contrast with the traditional 'voluntary' approach.

Professionalism and Development 'On the Job'

In reflecting on their experience of CPD, numerous interviewees argued that better planned INSET develops confidence, gives a sense of 'being more professional', and contributes to skills improvements. Poorly structured IN-SET was, however, 'marginal' and sometimes even detrimental to professional roles and responsibilities.

A substantial minority of interviewees emphasize the 'growing professionalism amongst the staff' which is stimulated by good quality INSET. Numerous comments, both in questionnaires and interviews, point to the way CPD helps them to think through 'new ideas', identify 'new practices', open 'new doors' and 'new horizons', gain 'greater inspiration', has 'improved morale' and 'reduces isolation'. Two senior manager interviewees also mention how their 'vision' of their role and place within the school improved as a result of longer-term CPD.

INSET was also deemed 'confirmatory' for a large minority of main scale teachers and middle managers: as one HOD said, it 'has helped to fine-tune general feelings', reaffirm skills, and reinforce confidence and professionalism. Despite the demise in long-term funded opportunities, several senior and middle managers emphasize 'the value of reading' which 'also gave me some insight into my own management skills and my philosophy and relationship with colleagues'. Furthermore, both middle and senior managers particularly asserted the need for reflection, to find 'time to reflect, theorize and put things into practice'.

Most interviewees feel that INSET does and should have a clear impact on professional confidence levels and on relationships between staff, especially when it brings about a better appreciation of other colleagues' roles and responsibilities. Many see CPD as an essential vehicle for safeguarding their professional roles from being undermined, particularly by lack of knowledge about current developments. This process is seen as cyclical: increased knowledge, understanding and skills produce spin-offs in increased personal confidence which in turn enhances professional roles, creating a 'virtuous CPD circle', leading to improved professional performance, whether in classrooms or elsewhere. Even so, a cautionary note is sounded by one teacher who suggests that INSET may have a mixed or even detrimental impact on an individual's sense of professionalism: high quality CPD could sometimes 'undermine because it shows the ideal'.

Reflection...

Has your own experience of CPD made you more confident professionally? Does your own experience reflect a 'virtuous CPD circle' or a 'vicious' one? Does your own professional 'timeline' – where you trace the chronological progression of your career and personal development – reflect a move through training to establish competence, towards a development-focus involving reflection and reflexivity in approach?

This opportunity for reflection cannot really be met by definitive answers! Nevertheless, the tension between 'professionalism' and 'training for a job' may have caused you some concern. Confidence in analysing problems, finding solutions and evaluating impact is rather different from the kind of training which enables you, for example, to teach reading or maths effectively. A progression is involved here which brings us to the key elements of 'age' and 'stage' with our initial focus as professionals establishing basic competences which then underpins the potentially broader and deeper personal agenda we are likely to construct as we mature professionally and become more confident about our professionality.

Careers, Promotion and CPD

A high proportion of staff in project schools said they were 'pragmatic' in their professional aspirations and approach to career development. While CPD had not necessarily 'fired ambitions' it often raised awareness of potential future opportunities as well as the likely pressures. Early but positive CPD experiences and career development opportunities were seen as highly influential in stimulating skills development and promoting 'can do' attitudes towards promotion. Several individuals recalled that where CPD was an early, positive influence, they had become more proactive and personally ambitious, consciously broadening professional horizons with clearer aspirations to succeed.

By contrast, less successful early experiences were often highly demotivating, especially where the degree of pressure on senior managers was also obvious to these more junior members of staff. Breadth and quality of initial CPD experience are, therefore, potentially highly influential in determining attitudes to promotion and future teaching success, with on-the-job opportunities created 'through acting roles' seen as invaluable practice. Such perceptions and the potential for high 'teacher wastage' rates during the early years of teaching, present major challenges for those managing NQT and teacher returner developments, as well as for national policy-makers faced with planning for an increased teaching force by the millennium.

Interviewees also suggest that effective CPD produces 'a major impact on competency and skills', with some arguing the merits of 'on-the-job' and job-related development opportunities. One middle manager, for example, notes that 'informal help given by senior teachers and the PDC is much more worthwhile and immediate'. Several HODs and heads of year, as well as younger staff, see their senior colleagues as useful formal or informal role models. However, they also stress how 'negative shadowing' experiences can be seriously detrimental to confidence and personal skills development, particularly when poor (senior) role models are the only ones available.

The dangers of assuming that 'somehow automatic links exist' between CPD and gaining promotion were also emphasized, since mistaken assumptions about the potential impact of INSET on career prospects 'can be highly demoralizing', creating difficulties in adjusting to the realities of teaching again. Since CPD responsibilities now rest with schools, individuals are increasingly responsible for identifying their own career development opportunities. However, a number of interviewees point to a concern that 'things shouldn't just be left to happen – we still really need the old advisory support in some ways'.

Different Departments, Different Perceptions?

There is a broad general consensus that HODs are crucial and influential in 'setting the professional tone', both as individuals within their departments and as a middle management group in their schools. They are perceived as occupying a central role in determining how far CPD is dismissed, marginalized or pursued by departments. Only a few interviewees argue that there are departmental differences in approach to CPD (with one suggesting that scientists are less open to new ideas and interpersonal skills development than others!), while almost all suggest that departmental attitudes are far more dependent on the HOD's personality, leadership qualities and vision. Subject allegiance is seen as largely uninfluential. One headteacher suggests, for example, that 'really good HODs stand out because they are broader in approach than their own discipline'.

A majority of interviewees see the quality of departmental leadership and vision as both crucial and highly variable, with the level of departmental involvement in CPD being influenced by:

- the HOD's leadership and change management skills (seen as the most crucial factor);
- the age profile and 'newness' of the department's staff;
- the legacy of CPD involvement within the department;
- the 'progressive' or 'traditional' nature of the department's professional outlook generally; and
- the degree to which the department has an innovatory reputation to maintain: whether it is seen as 'one of our key departments – leading developments'.

Both teachers and senior managers see heads of department as 'championing' departmental priorities and articulating departmental staff needs, reflecting O'Sullivan *et al.*'s (1988) comment that HODs are team leaders who 'must be partisan'. Some HOD interviewees nevertheless saw their own CPD leadership and facilitating role as 'limited' and teachers argue that HODs achieve highly variable degrees of success as CPD leaders. While some HODs were 'proactive', some failed to contribute fully to the INSET decision-making process. Where they were involved but had little personal commitment to CPD, they could be 'a block to progress' rather than a support for their staff. Echoing Earley and Fletcher-Campbell's findings (1989), two HODs said their limited involvement in CPD planning was attributable to time pressures and the fact that curriculum responsibilities were paramount for them – effectively moving CPD down the agenda.

While both senior managers and teachers saw the HOD role as a potential linking mechanism in relation to teacher development, almost a third of HODs interviewed emphasized their own needs for more support and training in both the content and process of staff development. A significant number also acknowledged that such a need was, at present, 'really rather low' on their own priorities list, partly because of other job-related pressures, but also because of lack of expertise and concern about raising false expectations in staff. Several HODs felt that staff development was not a major element in their role, though some accepted that this viewpoint may not longer be acceptable. Earley (1995) found a similar reluctance amongst middle managers to accept the notion of being a development 'protagonist', while Fielding (1996) stresses the importance of middle management training which enables HODs to provide more effective collegial support – an issue now also on the TTA agenda.

Harris *et al.* (1995) review the features of successful departments and register a series of factors which they suggest are seen as central to professional leadership, some of which are clearly linked to the HOD's role as a CPD facilitator:

- a focus on pupil/student achievement;
- systematic record-keeping;
- regularly scrutinized departmental results;
- a departmental change focus;
- the effective organization of departmental teaching;
- the value of professional support achieved through collegiality;
- the development of a shared vision; and
- a consistency in approach, encouraging low staff turnover.

The staff we interviewed perceive that this breadth of emphasis is growing, albeit slowly in some schools, as middle managers are progressively gaining status as pivotal agents for school improvement. One case study school, for example, runs its own 'Managing INSET' sessions as part of an induction course for all new HODs, with the PDC working as a mentor to new HODs in their first year of appointment.

Different Roles, Different Perceptions?

Intervewees show general unanimity of opinion over the ways in which senior managers and teaching staff perceive the value of CPD. For example, a majority of both teaching and senior staff interviewees consider school managers are often 'school-focused', 'concerned with whole-school issues' and 'driven by the SMT agenda' in their approach to CPD. In addition, however, senior managers were thought to have 'more of an eye to their own careers', to use CPD as 'a means to promotion', and to see CPD as a 'justifiable perk' or 'part of the job'.

More flexible timetables also meant senior staff undertook INSET when others couldn't. There was, nevertheless, general agreement that it was vital to 'get involved and show you're committed' to CPD, since it demonstrated 'a curiosity and interest in improving things' and a commitment to career. Several managers also note that while INSET is clearly part of their professional responsibility, it creates internal tensions. One head of faculty comments that, 'senior staff feel they have a responsibility to access knowledge and expertise, but are also reluctant to be away from the school', while one headteacher suggests that senior staff:

> have an obligation and duty to manage the overall strategic work of the school and therefore INSET is a tool in their overall armament to deliver tasks and efficiency… main scale staff have more of a local view of 'self' and 'department'.

There was also general agreement that main scale teachers were more 'subject-focused' and 'concerned with individual issues', perhaps partly because CPD was also 'a bit more of a scarce commodity' for them. While one middle manager argued that 'it is *my impression* that most main scale staff need to be pointed in the right direction', most interviewees saw no real differences in approach. For one headteacher it was more a case of 'the newer the role the more open to development', although some senior managers argued that the more limited responsibilities of main scale colleagues inevitably inhibit their knowledge of 'strategic and global issues' in education, which in turn influences their attitudes to professional development.

Different Gender, Different Perceptions?

While a minority of interviewees thought that men 'tend to be more promotion-minded', most interviewees felt that, overall, there was 'no clear difference' between men and women in their approach to CPD. Five women and three men, did, however, suggest there could be differences in perception asserting, for example, that men 'see CPD as a right, while women see it as their responsibility' and 'women tend to give up their own time more often, but men will often see it [CPD] as part of their job'.

The prevailing gender balance within both the senior management team and teaching staff in a school may create a skewed picture of CPD commitment and attendance, particularly, for example, where the SMT is predominantly male and retains the remnants of a gendered hierarchy in which women's' job descriptions tend to tie them to what are traditionally perceived as 'women's' tasks (Litawski, 1993). Despite evidence that, with the development of senior management teams, women are becoming less rigidly confined to stereotypical roles (McBurney and Hough, 1989; Wallace and Hall, 1994), a number of interviewees consider that career and professional development opportunities for women do appear to be becoming constrained within the more pressurized financial environment now facing schools, exacerbating existing difficulties in gaining release and promotion opportunities. One (male) headteacher suggests that the tight financial climate of school-based management career-blocks a number of women because, while 'many able women are now desperate to catch up on careers after family experiences, this is increasingly difficult as there is a financial imperative now to employ younger staff'.

A few men and several women interviewees also highlighted the issue of women's apparent lack of confidence in putting themselves forward for CPD experiences, both on and off-the-job, suggesting that women 'need to be pushed' but tend to be 'more thorough and critical' of potential openings. Men are perceived by many interviewees as generally more confident. Overall, however, there is a broad consensus that past INSET experiences, combined with on-the-job learning and support from middle and/or senior management, have a greater impact on CPD attitudes than does gender.

Institutional Costs and Benefits

Interviewees and staff in survey schools were asked to identify the institutional costs and benefits of INSET. Survey data collected over several years enabled some comparative analysis to take place and interviews provided a detailed picture of the perceived gains and losses facing schools and colleges.

Reflection...

Before you read this coming section and the following one (both of which review identified 'gains' and 'losses' for secondary and primary schools) try jotting down what you perceive to be the gains and losses arising from CPD within your own institution. Then consider how and in what ways your own list matches that which arises out of our research with schools.

Your response is likely to be a reflection of the past history of professional development and INSET within your own organization, as well as the management style(s) and culture(s) which have influenced its development activities, focus, and the availability of resources in support. As you read the following sections on gains and losses you may begin to identify the various positive and negative attitudes which arise out of the way in which CPD is managed in your own institution.

Gains and Losses for Secondary Schools

Senior management respondents in both the primary and secondary surveys were asked to identify what they saw as the key institutional benefits to be gained from CPD. Overall, secondary school respondents articulated a fuller range of benefits accruing from INSET than did primary schools. Table 5.1 summarizes what respondents saw as the key benefits to secondary schools.

Table 5.1 *Perceived benefits from CPD (secondary schools, 1995)*

Perceived benefits	Specific mentions
Organizational	
Increased whole-school awareness	18
Team building	6
Flexibility of planning	5
Updating	5
Unifying cohesion for school	3
Overall school development	3
Staff	
Increased staff skills/expertise	17
Improved staff efficiency	9
Networks developed	8
Personal professional development	7
Improved morale	6
Individual growth	6
Investors in People recognition	6
Increased confidence	4
Accreditation	2
Teaching and learning	
Curriculum development	12
Departmental growth	12
Improved quality of teaching	4
Achievement of SDP	4
Inspection preparation	4

Senior managers in the 1995 secondary survey echo concerns raised in 1994 and perceive that,

> we are building up a system which gives staff the view that they can have the training they need, but in reality we either cannot afford it or we are not prepared to have the disruption which it entails.

A comparison of comments on questionnaire returns and interview data shows that perceived advantages are more complex than Table 5.1 indicates. Although senior managers' comments on questionnaire returns and in interviews tend to focus on the whole-school impact of CPD activities, interviews with both main scale teachers and middle managers are more closely concerned with classroom performance. For subject teachers, success criteria tend to be based on knowledge gains and skills enhancement: 'to become a more effective teacher in my subject and thus to do more for the school as a whole'.

Inevitably, while much hangs on the perceptions of the person completing a survey, a comparison of 1994 secondary survey responses and open commentaries with those of 1995 shows a developing awareness of how CPD is impacting at all levels in institutions, revealed by comments like, 'more opportunity for us to use time to reflect on what we're doing in the classroom', 'an opportunity to work with others without the pressure of classroom demands', and 'clearer collaboration in planning and implementing change'.

In 1994, schools focused on the basic, practical problems they faced in establishing new INSET management practices; the 1995 survey articulates the complexities they face in meeting individual staff needs alongside school needs and the pedagogic demands of effective professional development. The problems specifically identified by secondary schools during 1995 are outlined in Table 5.2.

Table 5.2 *Perceived problems of CPD (secondary schools, 1995)*

Perceived problems	Specific mentions
Organization	
Underfunding as a constraint	12
Administration problems	8
Difficulties in matching school and individual needs	7
Quality variability	4
Securing value for money	3
Dissemination of courses/information	3
Matching school needs and providers	2
Lack of information	2

Table 5.2 continued

Perceived problems	Specific mentions
Staff	
Variable quality of supply staff	9
Resentment	7
Time taken by professional development	6
Additional pressure on workload	6
Teaching and learning	
Disruption to normal teaching	11
Lost LEA links which weaken support	5
Deficit model of provision	2

Overall, significant INSET problems appear to flow from funding difficulties (eg, increased administration, value for money concerns), disruption to teaching (eg, supply, pressures of workload issues), an inability to meet identified staff needs (eg, time, resentment, matching needs, dissemination) and purchaser-provider links (eg, quality, information issues, loss of LEA). Both open commentaries and interviews with secondary school staff confirm that work overload is perceived as particularly problematic in relation to CPD:

> one of the greatest difficulties for the PDC is in attempting to develop enthusiasm amongst colleagues who are resentful of yet more intrusions on their free time.

Gains and Losses for Primary Schools

Table 5.3 summarizes the perceived benefits of CPD identified by primary school headteachers and deputies during 1995. In line with 1994, INSET-related funding is seen as a way of supporting the general school budget rather than being specifically earmarked for CPD, perhaps partly because GEST and development budgets in the primary sector are often very small.

Table 5.3 *Perceived benefits of CPD (primary schools, 1995)*

Perceived benefits	Specific mentions
Meeting school and individual needs	14
School development planning and move towards targets	8
Inspiration, development of values, a school viewpoint	7

Table 5.3 continued

Perceived problems	Specific mentions
Control of budget, support school in other ways	5
Development of staff confidence and consistency	5
Development of skills and information	4
Reflection and review processes	3
Flexibility of planning	3
Development of networks within staff	3

Overall, primary school managers see site-managed INSET as bringing increased opportunities for improving staff cohesion and developing staff awareness of whole-school planning and policy development issues. However, concerns are also expressed over the 'need to balance the gains against the impact on the pupils when staff are absent'.

CPD administration requirements continue to be a concern, alongside frustrations regarding the way regulations may inhibit forward planning. Anxieties over balancing needs against diminishing funds are also more noticeable in 1995, with a higher proportion of schools critical of the costs of externally provided CPD. Table 5.4 shows the perceived problems identified by primary schools in 1995.

Table 5.4 *Perceived problems of CPD (primary schools, 1995)*

Perceived problems	Specific mentions
Costs in the light of diminishing funds	17
Administration issues	12
Quality problems, including staleness and irrelevance	12
Cost and availability of effective supply help	8
Lack of planning and feedback	6
Achieving balance between individual and school needs	5
Distance from providing centres	4
Lack of information, poor communications, cancellations	4

Alongside a reduction in the range and number of identified problems in primary schools in 1995 (for example, compared with 1994 there is less criticism of LEA provision) schools now appear to be 'much more in control of what we're doing' for CPD. Open commentaries suggest, however, that there is increasing concern over both content and delivery issues, with diminishing (though still substantial) worries about administration and the practicalities of distance, venue and environment.

Evaluating Institutional Gains

Although staff identify a wide range of personal and institutional gains, some are identified as being clearly linked with what they see as greater institutional flexibility arising from INSET funding and decision-making being delegated to organizations. These benefits are, however, seen as substantially constrained by 'environmental' limitations facing the organization and PDCs feel their room for manoeuvre is very limited, with funds and time 'getting more and more squeezed and we get left to deal with it… in the end we're the ones at the sharp end!' Despite these doubts, benefits are often perceived as outweighing problems. The main benefits identified as deriving from CPD and building a basis for future development in many schools can be clustered under the following headings:

- coherent planning and decision-making;
- improved staff skills;
- improved monitoring of provision;
- improved motivation and teamwork;
- an improved teaching and learning focus;
- a 'questioning culture';
- improved needs identification; and
- appraisal as professional support.

Coherent Planning and Decision-making

A high proportion of schools said they were developing 'more coherent planning procedures' which were generating improvements in the quality of CPD decision-making – though not necessarily the quality of provision used. There was a greater sense of 'ownership' of developments and even with the problems they faced, both managers and main scale staff feel that 'it's more under our control – and we can make choices – we can at least choose *how* we're going to go at things'. Senior staff felt that greater coherence had been stimulated by their control over decision-making and money, leading to 'people being more careful about what they choose'.

Improved Staff Skills

The development of school-managed CPD has often brought about, in many schools, the rise in status of the personnel deputy or PDC (particularly where budget responsibilities are attached to the role) alongside an increase in the in-house status of CPD. Senior staff also felt that staff skills were improving, particularly in relation to needs analysis and evaluating their own practices. However, this comment came predominantly from those who first, claimed their schools had organized their CPD system effectively, and second, where staff were 'kept informed' and shared in decision-making about new CPD developments and system changes. Staff in several schools perceived that CPD's higher profile was making training opportunities better valued and better targeted for skills development. This in turn helped them become 'better professionals', more capable of 'thinking through the issues'.

Improved Monitoring

While monitoring processes are generally regarded as 'unsophisticated' and 'limited' in many schools, many are attempting to pay closer attention (and time) to it. It is seen as 'paying off' in terms of improved quality and value for money: 'the basic quality of INSET has increased as we, the customers, have become more discerning'. In addition, monitoring is seen as encouraging a view that 'proficiency leads to efficiency and effectiveness', with more unified approaches, making people feel they are 'moving in the same direction'.

Improved Motivation and Teamwork

The development of 'an up-to-date motivated staff' was also acknowledged as a major CPD benefit, which also helped schools to develop a 'common purpose for staff' and, in the words of one interviewee, provided the 'institutional glue' needed for improvements. The opportunity to work as part of a team and chances for 'pooling and sharing of ideas' were regarded as crucial if there were to be institutional benefits. School-based INSET was seen as providing 'a chance to get beyond day-to-day problems', allowing all staff, including non-teaching staff, to contribute to strategic planning. In addition, improved motivation was seen as a major spin-off from well-run and well-targeted whole-school development.

An Improved Teaching and Learning Focus

CPD had encouraged staff to pay more attention to teaching and learning issues and to evaluate, in a more 'thoughtful' manner, the impact of their work with pupils. However, there was also a recognition that teaching, learning and evaluation issues required much more attention: in schools which had begun to operationalize a coherent review and evaluation process this focus was becoming clearer.

Closer attention to teaching and learning processes are also seen by both main scale and senior staff as encouraging a more considered view of their professional needs which, in turn, underpins improvements in their classroom and organizational management skills. Several managers pointed out that CPD was integral to what one headteacher called 'a culture of improvement' – one which recognized that 'teachers are important learners too' and where the focus is on 'everyone learning'.

A 'Questioning Culture'

One major benefit seen as a by-product of better organized CPD was the development of 'a more curious approach' and 'a questioning culture', where staff are beginning 'to scrutinize what's going on more than we used to'. There are numerous comments about professional development increasing 'coherence' and a 'thinking through' of issues, with managers noting that this made staff more 'positive, healthy and open to change'.

The development of this kind of questioning culture was very patchy across schools. Staff in some schools were reviewing existing practice by going back to first CPD principles, for example, by developing new and revised programmes for NQT development; by reviewing the way regular supply staff were used; by attempting to establish clearer structures in relation to CPD; by developing more straightforward systems for reporting on INSET; by developing open review of different professional practices (eg, between departments); and by establishing self-directed in-house programmes for middle managers.

Despite external pressures for greater financial and professional accountability, many schools are keen to evolve their own self-directed and self-evaluated strategies for professional development which incorporate individual needs within an overall organizational framework. The focus on self-directedness is backed by growing reservations about the limits of largely skills-focused cascade models of training. This idea of maintaining a sense of what could be called 'institutional self-directedness' is crucial because, as one PDC argues:

> we believe that we should be offering provision of quality with clear links to the school development plan in which evaluation of activities is an expected procedure and through which we are learning that mutual observation is a most helpful approach to individual improvement.

Improved Needs Identification

While schools differed widely in the degree of sophistication with which they approached the process of needs identification, there was a great sense of 'getting somewhere' when schools seemed able to link the determination of needs at individual levels with those seen as important to sustain the institution overall. However, the process was often recognized as potentially difficult, time-consuming and sometimes cumbersome to organize. When computerized record-keeping and an annual, straightforward and readily accessible needs audit had been introduced, school staff thought this was mutually reinforcing of both the appraisal process for them as individuals and the school's development planning strategies. Staff were, however, keen to ensure that the needs identification process and audit try 'to acknowledge that we have needs as people and not just as teachers in a school', so that development and training opportunities could be utilized which would hopefully 'meet more than one agenda... when it's possible'.

Appraisal as Professional Development

Though practices were variable between different institutions, in institutions where needs identification opportunities were well organized and appraisal was 'effective and supportive', staff feel they are 'being valued' and are more committed to 'a more professional approach'. At its best, teachers feel effective appraisal processes create a sense of mutual respect and appreciation and sense of being a key part of an organized, integrated team, showing that 'you feel you're valued for what you do – what you're achieving – and what you've got to offer the school and the kids'.

Appraisal is seen by many staff as, potentially, a significant contributor to integrated professional practice. Where it has worked well it is seen by the headteachers as fundamental to both personal and school development planning, although the TTA survey (Page and Fisher-Jones, 1995) notes how perceptions differ over the links between appraisal and professional development: while 63 per cent of headteachers who responded see the link, only 12 per cent of teachers do so.

Schools in our project were at very different stages in their use of appraisal as integral to CPD. Some teachers see it as 'a chance to let people know what you'd like to achieve' and 'an opportunity to get your message across', while others feel it 'can seem judgmental', raise false expectations, be disappointing and hasn't 'become part of the school yet'. Major concerns were expressed when appraisal targets had been used to identify individual needs linked with departmental and school plans, and were then not met because of a range of reasons, such as poor planning, poor prioritization, limited time or no funds.

Evaluating Institutional Costs

Despite the high value placed on INSET, a number of important negative perceptions are seen as limiting institutional (as well as personal) success, with 'costs' sometimes simply a negative reflection of benefits. Overall, secondary schools identified more CPD-related problems, though this may be because of their greater experience of school-managed INSET. Primary school feedback is, in addition, reliant on survey data. A significant theme is a growing frustration over the range and combination of pressures – when, for example, funding restrictions combine with limited time and professional overload to create institutional demoralization. One primary school headteacher sums it up:

> with a decreasing pot of money there is a lack of cover for absent staff matched by a growing unwillingness to attend courses in the teacher's own time and a lack of interest as a result of increasing workloads.

The main pressures and costs of CPD are identified as:

- time
- funding
- disruption to routines
- 'cumbersome bureaucracy' and 'system strain'
- inadequate monitoring and evaluation
- 'wasted investments' and 'lost opportunities'
- cynicism and resentment.

Time

Time was seen as a constraint in two major and almost contradictory senses. First, CPD both 'steals time from teaching, so it has to be good' and presents staffing replacement and supply problems – an issue often raised by senior staff responsible for arranging 'cover', but noted by a number of main scale staff as well. Second (and more mention was made of this) staff feel insufficient time is available for CPD because 'staff need time to work on and spread good ideas' and the 'development timetable creates significant stresses' on top of normal teaching timetables. A lack of 'appropriate' time was the most frequently mentioned concern both in interviews and survey returns in relation to 'informal' as well as 'formal' CPD.

Senior managers recognize time is a key resource for underpinning efforts at professional and institutional improvement. As one headteacher comments: 'staff are under a lot of pressure and yet weekends are much needed and precious… this means INSET can involve time away from pupils and it's hard to find a way round this'.

Funding

Three areas of concern are highlighted, reflecting the complex and in some ways, contradictory funding pressures facing staff and schools. First, staff recognized that it was expensive 'to fund teachers to be out of the classroom', but were equally keen that individuals should not be pressured to justify their participation – virtually all interviewees see INSET as a personal and professional entitlement. Second, what might be called the growing 'personalization of funding' was an issue for many staff, with a view that it was becoming too heavily skewed towards individuals self-funding their own development – a sense that 'nowadays you're on your own... unless it's for a some government initiative'. For many, frustrations were developing because funding underpinned other resources:

> The greatly increased range of provision in the last 10 years has coincided
> with considerably reduced funding. Staff expectations and needs are difficult
> to meet and time is rarely available to follow up the work.

Third, there was annoyance over 'inequitable funding levels' and the 'basic unfairness' of funding distribution – both between LEA schools and across the LEA-GM divide. Several PDCs and headteachers point to 'the great disparity between GM and LEA funding and this causes the staff of the erstwhile LEA schools to feel that they [GM schools] are gaining at the expense of others'.

Even though both primary and secondary schools accept that the overall quality of INSET and CPD has improved in certain respects (eg with devolution of decision-making and funding to institutions), insufficient funding is regarded as a growing threat to existing achievements and further development.

Disruption to Routines

The way professional development disrupts school and teaching routines is viewed as a longstanding problem by many staff, but one which has been exacerbated by the rapid changes being implemented in schools. Senior staff responsible for replacement and supply provision as well as teaching staff, comment on how CPD creates teacher overload through disrupted teaching patterns, produces 'even more preparation and then marking of set work when I get back', and creates the psychological stresses of 'catching up' and 'coping with the overload'. Staff are, in addition, particularly concerned about the quality of pupils' learning when teachers in several departments are away simultaneously and 'the same group of kids suffer'.

'Cumbersome Bureaucracy' and 'System Strain'

A number of staff working in a range of professional roles argue that the impact (if not the principle) of accountability is developing an overly 'cumbersome bureaucracy' which, too often, 'ties up the PDC' with 'INSET book-keeping'. 'System strain' was seen as a major issue. The closer focus on accountability has made effective planning, monitoring and evaluation procedures even more crucial. Existing procedures are often seen as barely adequate and sometimes 'not even up to the task' and while 'paper procedures' exist, sometimes developed in anticipation of OFSTED inspections, communication difficulties between staff means that system strain becomes a major concern.

Some staff suggest that management responsibilities are insufficiently clear in their schools, leading to poorly or even inadequately focused planning, dissemination and review procedures. In addition, internal systems are seen as becoming strained because external support is no longer available 'on tap'. Although the majority of schools remain keen to control their own INSET and generate their own in-house support, anxieties also remain over 'how much more the system can take' and the fact 'the demise of teachers' centres has left us without a common local meeting ground where networks can develop'.

Inadequate Monitoring and Evaluation

Anxieties over monitoring and evaluation procedures as part of the general system strain are exacerbated where teachers feel they are being 'pushed into irrelevant courses which develops antagonisms' and where a course is 'demotivating if it was poor quality'. Staff feel that the demands on PDCs mean that too little time is spent on developing effective monitoring procedures. However, they are also sympathetic over the extent and complexity of the task facing PDCs – 'a thankless and never-ending task'. Evaluation was also seen as a weak element in CPD management – though it was accepted a whole-staff approach was required. Despite criticisms, interviewees felt that setting up effective evaluation processes was such a complex issue that they had little hope of remedying such problems quickly.

'Wasted Investments' and 'Lost Opportunities'

These related concerns were particularly highlighted by middle managers and main scale staff, who feel that their 'personal investments' as well as school-supported CPD is not always fully utilized; in effect, 'skills are just getting wasted'. While money is not a motivating factor for most staff, the lack of incentives and even limited rewards is perceived negatively. 'Doing a job which needs to be done' is no longer sufficient reward for many, particularly younger staff. Several interviewees also pointed to the pressures of parental and governors' concerns that, with reduced school budgets, any available money 'should go on the children'.

Staff very much regret their 'lost opportunities' where, for example, needs are identified and remain unmet or are only met pragmatically in order to ensure 'the money gets spent up before the end of the year'. Several point to their sense of being 'victims' of increasing organizational (and funding) constraints; as one senior manager admits, 'the greatly increased range of provision has coincided with considerably reduced funding – and staff expectations (following appraisal targets) are difficult to meet'.

Cynicism and Resentment

Endemic cynicism and resentment is perceived to be a relatively small but growing problem, especially amongst main scale staff. A wide range of potential demotivators are offered as contributory factors, including, for example, the fact that appraisal 'promises' often don't become professional development 'realities'; poorly targeted and negative INSET experiences add to rather than resolve other professional pressures; innovation fatigue and change exhaustion has become endemic; teacher support mechanisms are no longer available now that LEAs have stopped being professional 'release valves'; increasing evidence of teacher stress and ill-health, with ill health retirements doubling in a decade which seems indicative of a potentially negative future (*Education*, 1996); and OFSTED's and the media's focus on 'failing teachers' and 'failing schools' lowers self-esteem. In the light of such pressures, a number of staff pointed out that it is now easier to get bound into a 'spiral of professional negativity', where INSET is effectively an inadequate remedy faced with an impossible task.

Two teachers pointed out that even good quality INSET experiences could create resentment and cynicism, where CPD is too 'demanding' and 'unsettling' and individuals are made to confront changes which, in some ways, they would prefer to ignore. For some, the effect of government-directed changes 'on a largely mature workforce has been to cause cynicism and resentment which has undermined professional autonomy' and, as one PDC admits, 'we have never cracked those who don't want to take part and we have never got enough money to support those who do!'

Several senior managers note that 'cynicism remains with a minority of staff who see all training as an infringement of their freedom as professionals' and suggest that the pressures of 'training fever' flowing from government initiatives has provided a framework for resentment: In effect, both external pressures (such as revisions to the National Curriculum and inspection demands) as well as internal demands for change ('there are always new initiatives being developed') have led some teachers to feel that the development effort is not worth it.

Moving Towards Integrated Practice

If schools are to do their best for both students and staff, top-down and bottom-up initiatives need to become better integrated and merged (Fullan, 1991; 1993). Externally driven imperatives for change to curriculum and management practices imposed on schools and colleges during the last decade are now being replaced or complemented by increasingly sophisticated in-house change and development strategies, so that teacher development enhances pupil achievement.

As a consequence, schools are moving, albeit at very different rates, along a sometimes painful professional path towards identifying and then evaluating their CPD policies and examining their in-house practices. The more confident schools are progressively establishing embryonic and integrated professional development frameworks and many are concluding that without change brought about through teacher development, the scope for student and pupil development remains very limited.

The importance of a supportive development framework should not be minimized but must not be overemphasized. Fullan (1993) suggests that if schools are to be effective learning organizations which 'neither ignore nor attempt to dominate their environments', they will need to adopt 'new approaches to control and accountability'. He argues that 'learning organizations are more holistically accountable as they work more systematically'. The ability of organizations to learn also depends, however, on their capacity to 'manage the unknowable' (Stacey, 1992) and to manage change and 'thrive on chaos' (Peters, 1988) by building a supportive development climate capable of meeting a wide range of needs and demands. The challenge is to ensure that room is available for both structure and flexibility, for accountability and autonomy, and for individuality and collegiality so that the inevitable tensions which arise between collaborative and individualistic approaches can become productive rather than destructive (Fullan and Hargreaves, 1992).

The last decade has seen an increasing focus on performance indicators and success criteria in education and a growing concern to formalize CPD accountability processes. Darling-Hammond and Ascher (1992) point out that:

performance indicators... are information for the accountability system; they are not the system itself. Accountability (ie, responsible practice and responsiveness to clients) occurs only when a useful set of processes exists for interpreting and acting on the information (p.2).

Following Darling-Hammond and Ascher's suggestion, the 'useful set of processes' now becoming established to make CPD more accountable within the UK might be seen as including:

- the inception of frequent (four-yearly) OFSTED inspections of teaching and learning quality;
- the establishment of governing body responsibility for reporting on schools' professional development days;
- alterations in funding patterns to encourage the establishment of an 'IN-SET marketplace', incorporating provider-purchaser relationships and an expectation that value for money is a central focus;
- a devolved and more tightly administered GEST financial framework heavily focused on national priorities;
- a requirement that LEAs become responsible for monitoring post-OF-STED action planning linked to schools' improvement strategies;
- the establishment of the TTA, with an emphasis on increased competency and accountancy/accountability approaches to CPD;
- the developing requirement that CPD providers register with the TTA, agree to inspection and centrally controlled and formalized evaluation procedures of their programmes (eg, HEADLAMP) if they wish to benefit from government funded initiatives.

The increasing accountability focus is seen by some school staff as undermining 'the real tasks of teaching and learning' and 'distracting us from the key job we have': many suggest the balance between accountability and autonomy is not yet right. For example, one deputy head notes that:

> much of the current provision is functional rather than inspirational. Staff do not always enjoy courses in the same way that they did, partly because they know that they will have to come back to school to foster the cascade approach, and partly because courses are concerned with doing a task rather than thinking about its significance.

Consequently, a key task for schools is to utilize the best of what they have learnt in managing the functional changes over recent years in order to reinvigorate the inspirational aspects of their role. The need is to move beyond training fever and ad hoc provision towards managing a more coherent and integrated framework of institutional development where space also exists for individual professional autonomy. Chapter 6 examines the ways in which three schools are endeavouring to manage this process, while Chapter 7 offers a potential route towards building a professional development culture which enhances school, group and individual progress.

Reflection...

Is your own institution still focused on managing an externally imposed agenda for change or has it also begun to establish its own in-house priorities and strategies? What might be done to ensure that both the functional and the inspirational aspects of development are adopted in your own and your institution's approach to CPD?

CHAPTER 6

Professional Development in Practice:
Three Case Studies

These three exemplars of professional development practice in schools have been evolved following research by questionnaire and interview. They offer some hard evidence about the way in which context affects the approach taken to professional development; the way in which philosophy conditions practice; and the way in which professional development has an impact on stakeholders within the school. Besides giving factual detail, these studies also demonstrate the progression of professional development:

- from *ad hoc and random* opportunities to *planned and evaluated* ones;
- from *incoherent* episodes to *coherent* planning;
- from a *training* culture to a *professional development* culture; and
- from *isolated and individualized* development to *integrated and holistic* development.

Some understanding of the ways in which CPD policy makers within schools have responded to their environment can be a valuable aid in determining the precise nature of their practice. These anonymous case studies offer opportunities for reflection on the various strategies and philosophies employed by schools.

They offer some practical detail of the variety of school management practices in relation to INSET and personal and professional development and may also be helpful in reviewing the appropriateness of alternative institutional climates. Each of the schools recognizes that they are moving along a path towards a cultural change and that, for a variety of reasons, they are moving at differing speeds. The key element focused on in these case studies is not the practical detail itself, but rather the context and response; and it is this which is taken up in Chapter 7 where a typology of practice is offered as a potential 'professional development *aide-mémoire*'.

Case Study 1: Downlands School

This school reflects an evolving professional development culture, with evidence of changing staff attitudes. Whole-school policy is increasingly driven by the strategic aims of the school and senior staff recognize the importance of the integration of staff development as an essential prerequisite for progress. There is a developing coherence in planning and provision but, overall, arrangements continue to be pragmatic, randomized and poorly evaluated.

The Context

This is a semi-rural comprehensive and co-educational 11–16 school with 725 pupils and 43.2 full-time equivalent staff. It is situated in an area where schools are in competition and where the cachet of GM status in nearby schools has led to some loss of pupils who would normally attend the school. At the same time, the school is gaining from other LEA schools in the locality. The social mix of the school has changed over the past ten years with the development of private housing and a concurrent rise in the expectations of parents. The school is supported by an active PTA and there is strong community use of its premises.

The school was formerly a secondary modern, but has been comprehensive for so long that this fact does not appear to influence public perceptions of what is offered any longer. However, the higher expectations of the increasing owner-occupier community does present a challenge for the head and staff in planning strategic development: academic results are now seen as being extremely important by staff and a necessary focus of development activities.

While there is, in general, a shared involvement of all staff in decision-making, there is also a recognition that certain issues have to be decided by the senior management team. However, a cycle of meetings at head of department and head of year level, followed by subject and year team meetings, and then followed by a full staff meeting ensures that matters of principle and policy are thoroughly aired within the institution.

There is considerable delegation of decision-making to departments where this is considered to be more effective. In relation to professional development matters, the senior management team establishes broad policy, but the overall responsibility rests with the recently appointed staff development coordinator (SDC) for whole-school issues and with the head of department or head of year for team activities. The establishment of consistent practice is now a recognized priority of the senior management team. Current whole-school aims are:

- an improvement in classroom practice;

- the development of more effective monitoring policies; and
- the raising of individual teacher skill levels.

These aims are illustrated in the development programme for one department which has undertaken the rewriting of KS 3 and the development of IT skills as a basis for departmental skills development. This department has used £700 during the past year, 'mainly on supply staff' to allow full departmental meetings. An attempt is now being made to evaluate each of the varied approaches to development being used within the school.

The school does not have a strong history of professional development. Indeed, 'a culture of involvement is really only just developing'. Some staff would not be involved if the management 'didn't push it' and there is a prevailing view that where staff have reached their current level of promotion or status there is no need for further personal improvement. Professional development is, therefore, linked in peoples' minds to career progression rather than to general school improvement. In the head's view, 'staff are not customer oriented enough because there's no intrinsic reward'. By contrast, however, those who are keen to use professional development seem to value it highly and acknowledge the efforts made by the staff development deputy to meet their requests.

The local educational environment does not appear to be conducive to staff or professional development. Schools have made no attempt to work together in planning or delivering INSET programmes, partly because schools are in competition, but also because there is no tradition of local coordination. There is also a feeling within the school that too much of the possible funding for professional development is still held centrally and that the LEA prospectus is not really appropriate to meet the particular needs of individual schools.

Planning and Practicalities

Professional development opportunities are managed by the deputy responsible for staff development. All information is channelled through him to the staff, either via personal contact or through using the staff room's dedicated noticeboard. INSET material is generally kept in a ring binder for future reference. Sometimes, specific information may go directly to heads of department through LEA or other consultancy mailing lists.

Proposed programmes of activities are discussed either directly by individuals or by heads of department or year with the deputy head. The criterion for acceptance onto a course or activity is that it should be relevant to the agreed school development plan or departmental plans. There is some flexibility in arrangements to allow for changes in INSET needs and any late notification of suitable opportunities by the LEA.

Financial allocation from the LEA is limited to GEST funding, at about £8,000 in 1995, and supplemented from the school budget, with about £1,500 in the current year. All identified whole-school priorities are allocated a notional sum and this is then further divided between departments according to the range of needs outlined for, and accepted by, the senior management team.

The SDC maintains a database which tracks expenditure and from which possible development activities can be identified. The database is also used to provide details of individual, departmental and whole-school participation in activities. Forward spending is programmed in March each year. However, although the global limits are maintained, planned expenditure by priorities rarely turns out as predicted because of the dynamic and sometimes unpredictable nature of development. Staff commend this flexibility as a positive feature of current organization but the SDC feels that this actually acts as an inhibitor in strategic planning.

Relationships with LEA personnel in the advisory service are variable and depend on individual relationships according to subject area. All schools submit their staff development plans to the advisory team and in this way the LEA's programme of activities is at least theoretically influenced by the needs of the schools. The school also has a link adviser, who ensures that school needs are transmitted to the relevant subject advisers. The school most frequently uses advisers for monitoring, review and evaluation and to provide specialist input for departmental and year activities. To ensure that the service is effective – because 'after all we do pay for it!' – the school tries to plan ahead and make arrangements with each of the advisers who it is believed can offer them particular expertise.

The school does not make use of local HEI provision, but does use private consultancy where the service has a reputation for quality and provides good venues. While the cost is perceived to be high, senior staff argue that the value for money is good. The school provides opportunities for staff to develop individual skills through work with peers either as part of the timetable or with inservice time allocation.

In addition, the school is involved in initial teacher education and training with a university. While the school makes no use of the HEI for its professional development, senior staff acknowledge that the relationship brings new ideas into the associated departments and promotes a degree of personal critical reflection on teaching and learning strategies and classroom practice since 'it challenges perceptions and opens up new ideas for discussion'.

Whole-school priorities are established by using a review of the previous year as part of the school development planning process. Many themes, such as differentiation and assessment, are ongoing but others arise in response to advisory evaluation and national initiatives. Departments review progress in the same way in order to evolve departmental development plans. The head of department then discusses departmental needs with the staff development deputy head in order to produce a draft staff development plan. Both school and staff development plans are then discussed at departmental and whole-staff level before final ratification. This formalization of planning is resulting in a more precise and organized overall programme. Administration is managed by the staff development deputy aided by an administrative assistant who tracks expenditure and maintains the database.

Evaluation has not been fully developed either at whole-school or departmental level. At present, it is heavily reliant on word-of-mouth comments on course content, delivery and involvement but some formalization of the process is presently under consideration. Both school and departmental development plans incorporate success criteria and performance indicators and a number of departments make use of these to assess the value of INSET experiences in meeting aims.

The Impact

Professional development is undertaken in a variety of forms. Staff most commonly attend courses and inservice days as 'basic INSET', but also mention meetings held off-timetable as well as attendance at off-site meetings for examination moderation and similar activities. Departmental review and evaluation is acknowledged as a developmental opportunity as are meetings with advisers to establish and promote new initiatives. While the head considers that the professional development culture within the school remains rather limited, there is evidence that it is developing, since 'we have moved from courses to use departmental reviews as our starting point to improve what's actually happening in the classroom'.

Despite the idea that staff are 'unwilling participants' initially, there is a prevailing view that professional development is being appreciated for what it does to assist school development. The benefits in classroom practice are balanced against the loss of time while staff are participating in courses and the disruption which 'seems to hit some pupils more than others by coincidence'. It is felt that some staff are more unwilling than others to provide cover for colleagues involved in INSET activities – 'usually those staff who do not want to get involved in development activities themselves'.

A number of staff feel that a professional development culture is developing, particularly as increasing numbers of colleagues become involved and begin to identify a close link between training and the needs identified within the school development plan. This they feel is a spur to further involvement.

The high status accorded to activities by the staff development deputy and the use of a system which 'appears fair. I've never been refused and the staff development plan is costed and open to everyone', contributes to the embryonic development culture.

That said, more comprehensive development is hampered by inadequate funding, by the perceived lack of value-for-money courses and by an unwillingness of several staff to be absent from the classroom. Some staff do not appear to understand the way in which the plan is developed or the part which they themselves might play in influencing policy. Neither do they seem to understand or be interested in the financial allocation procedure. There is no dissatisfaction in the reported responses to requests to meet needs and the current system is generally commended for three features: it is based on identified priorities which have significance at all levels in the school; it is a product of the school planning cycle; and it is handled by a development deputy who is aware of the competing demands and the ways in which these may be met.

Case Study 2: Hillside School

In this school progress towards a coherent professional development policy is driven by the need to meet the targets identified within the school development plan. Basic needs analysis is obtained through departmental requests, appraisal and senior management discussions with the staff. The opportunity to reconcile personal and whole-school needs is inhibited by a somewhat diffuse management of activities.

However, the responsibility for aspects of professional development is shared between the two deputy headteachers and there is a commonly agreed, though unpublished, policy which aims to encourage development in all aspects of school organization. Opportunities have evolved within a range of activities which are now being evaluated in a simple way as a guide to future policy and practice.

The Context

The school is a comprehensive, LEA maintained 11–18 co-educational school of 652 pupils serving a small market town and the associated scattered rural communities. Some pupils come to the school from more distant small towns. Forty-two staff now work on an improved site opening onto extensive playing fields on the edge of the town. The buildings have been developed from the former secondary modern school with recent, high quality additions following the closure of the former grammar school, situated in the town, which had become the lower school following comprehensive reorganization.

Community expectations of the school are high and relationships are good, with recent efforts to increase access to the site and its facilities. There is some payback from this in that parental support is also strong with a high degree of involvement. From a professional development viewpoint, for example, the availability of volunteer invigilators during the main exam period has allowed departmental and other working groups to undertake extensive planning in addition to the other training and development opportunities; this year 300 staff hours were made available in this way.

At the same time, there is strong parental pressure on staff to ensure that pupils succeed, often without a realistic understanding of the range of abilities and the difficulties of organizing the curriculum and support within a comparatively small school. Results at GCSE equate with the average for all comprehensive schools and A-level scores are slightly above average. Staff are aware that in a situation where there is considerable competition between schools, many of the more academic children may be moved to schools in the county town unless results are seen to be good. The school is receptive to parental and community opinion and encourages participation in social, money-raising and cultural events. There is good governor involvement in the school and the strategic aims of growth through increased recruitment at Year 7 and the development of a broad range of sixth form opportunities are of fundamental importance to school development planning.

The school is in the fourth year of a restructured management organization which is based around a senior management team comprising the head and two deputies, and a broader management team known as the school development committee, which is based on heads of department and the pastoral heads in the school. Over the past four years, the headteacher has been keen to ensure that administrative systems are in place and understood and that a system which encourages consistent whole-school practice exists. As a result all departmental meetings, for example, are set up with an agenda, reports, papers and minutes which are available to the senior management team to monitor developments and to provide a framework for subsequent discussion.

The school development plan evolves out of school development committee discussions of whole-school priorities, supplemented by departmental development plans which show how these policies are being interpreted. This sets the professional development and budget planning parameters for the coming year. The staff also establish their personal targets through appraisal, either with their head of department or a pastoral equivalent, and efforts are then made to consider these in planning to meet whole-school and departmental needs.

Staff feel that they are able to express their views on possible training opportunities or school needs but 'generally there is a top-down movement of suggestions because the head understands what he needs to do for the

133

school in a period of change'. The senior management team's shared management philosophy is reflected in the easy way in which deputies share their professional development responsibilities. One deputy looks after initial teacher education and induction, while the other is responsible for appraisal and course attendance. The team as a whole plan the school's professional development or training days but delegate by allocating about one and a half training days to departments each year. All planning is confirmed with the head following consultation with the staff development committee in matters of policy development and implementation.

The school is involved in an initial teacher education scheme with a local college of higher education, taking four students a term. It also supports an Open University PGCE student. Increasing use is being made of in-house training programmes using the expertise of a group of staff for reflection and development planning, but recognizing the need to offer some stimulation by using external people to prompt new thinking. These consultants are usually known LEA contacts or come from subject or professional networks. The close relationship with the LEA is still maintained, but is not as evident as it was in the days before the funds were devolved to the school. Freedom to purchase help from alternative sources is leading to a more discriminating approach.

There is a common view that, over recent years, attitudes to professional development have changed: 'INSET was just an add on... and professional development was for other people – it was yet another burden on what we did as teachers'. There may be some limited, but continuing, resistance to whole-school development, but recent opportunities have been much valued. The strategy adopted when the head was first appointed was to build involvement through achieving evident successes from a staff volunteer working group which had investigated the relationship between pastoral care and teaching and learning priorities.

In this work, TVEI money was used to fund intensive on-site training followed by continuing on- and off-site sessions which involved developing counselling skills. The success of this prompted a further cohort to undertake training, and this established a pattern of working groups assisted by outside consultants wherever possible. The head's view is that staff should be given the best possible environment for professional development support and that some limited finance should be used to pay for refreshments/consumables.

While the evolution of a professional development culture has moved forward, the head feels that this must now move towards a more comprehensive and collective vision of what the school should aim for. This supersedes present concerns with development according to the strategic plan which is partly marketing-driven. The impact of the OFSTED inspection process on the normal progress of professional development is mentioned as a 'way of moving forward on the things that we ought to have been doing, but also an inhibiting factor in that the school was being driven by outside pressures'.

At departmental level, the legacy of action-planning to meet the National Curriculum requirements has affected the way in which priorities are viewed. Limited LEA help has given individuals and groups a number of ideas and materials, but real development is dependent on middle management leadership. Senior staff feel that OFSTED has hindered rather than helped the development of an integrated, whole-school development culture.

Planning and Practicalities

The school's CPD budget is 'used flexibly to maximize the opportunities for staff' and although the allocated GEST sum is modest (as is all funding within this predominantly rural county) about half of this sum is used for books and materials to support curriculum development. A further sum of about £4,000 is allocated from the school budget to meet all courses, training day expenses and consultancy for departmental development. Little use is made of the LEA in this respect since most subject advisers are now fully committed either to OFSTED inspection preparation and follow-up or as part of inspection teams. Until 1995, the travel budget has met INSET costs but 'real costing' means that from now on it will be attributed to professional development costs. Purchasing for all development work is however guided by the need to secure value for money within a modest budget.

Courses are used wherever these 'offer what we think that we need but we have to balance the costs of travel and the likelihood of it not being what we want against the reputation of the provider'. Permission to attend courses/events may result from discussions between any of the deputies, the heads of department and the individual staff, with decisions usually based on curriculum development needs or known targets emanating from appraisal, or simply from the identification of a need by an individual which had become known to others. There appears to be only a limited need for formality within a comparatively small staff and the arrangements for attendance and funding are settled with one deputy and arrangements made for cover with the other. Both deputy heads therefore appear to be aware of what is being undertaken by individual staff. Publicity for courses is available either from the LEA booklet, which is criticized for its late publication when the senior staff have to begin the planning to meet SDP needs ahead of the year in question, or from the numerous flyers 'which we feel may be valuable to those who know the providers, or where we've had previous good experiences, but generally are an unknown quantity for us – given our comparative isolation and lack of close association with any HE institution'.

Evaluation post-attendance rests largely on word-of-mouth to senior staff creating a body of opinion about what is available, and by reporting back to departmental meetings although this is not always a major item in the agenda. There is agreement that a more robust evaluation procedure is needed for noting information on course quality and content, and for subsequent departmental use. However, 'with heavy administrative burdens we don't want to create a chore where the bureaucratic output might be cosmetic or of limited value when so much will probably change'.

There has been a tendency to use consultants as a means of obtaining ideas to feed into in-house debates and development. This has occurred recently in relation to new arrangements for sixth form learning patterns, developed following three lengthy 'planning change' twilight sessions for all staff, supported by LEA and other external expertise. In-house arrangements predominate at departmental level and have been determined in part by responses to OFSTED and by the need to respond to constantly changing curriculum orders.

Departmental developments have been helped by senior management support for departmental planning meetings during the summer term and by the need for departments to respond to changing emphases on several cross-curricular issues, as well as the need to adapt teaching and learning styles. The balance of training days allows an additional one and a half days for departments and three days for whole-school issues. These are intended to develop priorities established as fundamental to all areas of the school which have been identified as a result of development planning – 'differentiation approaches' has been a recent theme picked up within the English department, for example, and now planned to move into consideration of reading and writing policies on a whole-school front.

Appraisal has recently been reviewed after the first round of operation and there is now greater flexibility in determining the basis of evaluation and the nature of the appraisal. The sharing of established targets with members of the senior staff is seen as fundamental to effective personal professional development and while the process has been useful, some staff have felt that 'given our limited funds, we know we can't demand more than can realistically be met, and sometimes we lose individual needs because we're aware of what's wanted for the department'.

At the same time, staff appreciate the efforts made by the deputy heads to secure opportunities to meet training needs in support of the school development plan. Broad acceptance of this as a way of prioritizing requests appears to be leading staff to develop their own set of priorities based on what they need to do – essentially a development perspective. Targets established during appraisal form the basis of individual development planning, but the deputy head comments that 'as with so many things it's difficult to maintain any sort of mapping which properly records the way individual, departmental and school needs are being met – after all, one opportunity sometimes satisfies several needs!'

Staff are enthusiastic about the participation of the school in an extended initial teacher education scheme. Student teachers are placed in the subject areas in pairs during the autumn term while developing planning, delivery and class management styles in small teams associated with the normal class staff, and then a further four students follow a fuller teaching programme in four subject areas with mentors during the spring term. Positive advantages are seen to be that the mentors gain from the experience; the students are given support while developing their skills in a way which causes teaching staff to reflect on their own practice; the staff concerned are led to focus upon their own and other teaching approaches and develop their skills of communication and persuasion; and the responsibility given to the mentor enhances his or her own development.

The involvement of one deputy head as professional mentor also enhances the team organization and provides further opportunities for reflection and development based upon needs identified while working with trainee teachers. This additional funding also allows for some development financing within departments and the school, and the evolution of mentoring skills is reflected in the care at whole-school and departmental level in the induction of newly appointed staff.

The Impact

The senior management team believes that their evolving INSET scheme is based on staff needs in support of the development plan. By identifying strategic needs they believe their view of the school over the next two or three years enables them to establish the broad basis of development. They are aware that there will be a need to adapt in order to respond to changing priorities and that changes to funding and administrative arrangements may affect staff opportunities. Heads of department are also aware of 'the direction the school is going in and are trying to reconcile this with subject development needs so that there's less distinction between departmental and whole-school development'.

Lack of funding is a major problem compared with GM schools. Where staff need 'time, opportunity and expertise in order to develop' there are grave problems in meeting both the personal and school targets identified in

OFSTED and appraisal processes. The need for some form of audit, both of needs and opportunities, is also recognized, but staff feel increased bureaucracy to achieve value for money may be detrimental in terms of time.

However, some meetings are seen as 'professional development by another name... the school should record these opportunities' and it is suggested that the main thrust of change should be by 'making professional development central to all development planning – one can't exist without the other, and both need time for reflection'. The deputy heads responsible for staff development are aware of this and new budgetary systems are enabling them to identify real costs for a variety of meetings.

There is no doubt that declining LEA opportunities are keenly felt by staff because of lost personnel to conduct subject, pastoral or whole-school courses, and the consequent loss of networking with staff elsewhere. The school does, however, endeavour to meet all requests if they are justified by the school or department needs and if they provide value for money, as well as some gain to individuals. The use of examiners' meetings as a substitute for other forms of development training is recognized as one of the few remaining ways in which the school can support staff at minimum cost.

While the deputy heads support requests at all levels as fully as they can within the constraints of course costs and supply staffing needs, they are also aware of 'disruption costs' to lesson continuity and staff–pupil relationships. The quality, support and involvement of a team of supply staff is good and the impact on classes in the event of staff absence is minimized. However, 'we can only guess at the impact of all the out-of-class demands and student involvement on any one individual'. The head and deputy heads have made achieving the SDP and personal development needs clear priorities within the budgetary framework, but staff are also very concerned that absence should only be allowed when it is in the interests of pupils and follows assessment of the impact of the request against the added value to pupils' learning. Put another way 'it's essential that we minimize disruption which could affect results – but then weekends and twilight sessions have their impact on us as professionals and people and it's a matter of balance'. Changes in initial teacher education procedures have minimized one source of disruption because the new scheme enhances classroom management before students develop whole-class teaching. The mentor's responsibility is also more immediate and effective if there are signs of weak teaching.

The need to use limited resources wisely and according to criteria related to the SDP may give staff an impression of top-down management – a view taken by some heads of department who may not always feel in control, because they do not share the same concern to develop a whole-school framework over tutorial work and pastoral care, for example. Teaching staff are not always aware 'why we're following a particular theme and feel that they're subject to external influences' rather than part of proactive developments based on widely agreed needs. When asked to suggest how these problems could be overcome, it was felt that the head was still engaged in 'redefining the direction of the school' as well as the necessary staff development to achieve this. However, in practical terms some more thorough auditing and evaluation was thought to be beneficial in promoting value for money.

Where frustrations occur they are usually connected with the loss of individual CPD opportunities and a realization that appraisal may be setting up unrealistic targets which either conflict with whole-school or departmental policies, may not be supportable, may relate only to individual opportunities which might not meet school needs, or may fail to give individuals the necessary sense of empowerment for success. All these are common feelings when staff are asked to indicate their personal needs within a corporate system. The senior management team recognizes that, within the limitations of the existing framework, they attempt to achieve a balance between school, department and individual, and between academic and pastoral objectives. They do this by seeking professional development opportunities which 'give the best VFM in our circumstances, meet the greatest number of needs and help us to work towards the SDP'.

Staff feel that the most important element in meeting individual needs at present is through closer links with higher education. This might provide accreditation for in-house development so that opportunities are seen by staff as more than just 'getting the tools to do the job'. To this end, the proposed integration of the major facets of professional development into one published policy might strengthen awareness of the responsiveness to staff needs through every possible opportunity. This is jointly and openly managed by the deputy heads, but still seen by some staff as compartmentalized. As a result, achieving a development culture is inhibited.

Case Study 3: Oxbury School

Professional development in this school has been reorganized following the move to GM status. Needs analysis, planning of opportunities for development, evaluation and finance are all managed by one deputy head with responsibility for all personnel functions.

Staff are increasingly aware of the benefits of professional development and recognize that a culture exists which promotes individual, departmental and whole-school growth. All activities are carefully evaluated and thorough records are used by the Staff Development Committee, which works with the deputy head, to produce a coherent annual calendar of activities.

The Context

The school is a seven-form entry, 11–18 comprehensive school, situated in a suburban village midway between two large towns and drawing from a wide suburban and rural catchment area. It had been a grammar school which reorganized as a comprehensive, but which retains many features of the ethos of the former school. The fact that examination results show over 60 per cent of pupils gaining five or more higher grade GCSE and an average A-level score of 17 points makes it a highly desirable school locally and it currently refuses admission to around 40 pupils a year because of accommodation constraints and the decision that to grow further would be detrimental to the quality of education on offer.

Intake is monitored for its geographical dispersion and the quality of pupils' cognitive abilities on entry as a means of developing a value-added analysis and to give a basis for teaching and learning assessments. Changes within the existing grammar schools in the nearby city may lead to some 'creaming' of intake. The school has a strong sporting and, latterly, music tradition with annual productions and concerts in the nearby cathedral . It is a 'school which has got everything going for it… a good place to work and with marvellous youngsters'.

Parental expectations are high for both academic achievement and personal development and there is strong support for a firm uniform policy, activities, and funding. The PTA is the strongest community element drawing on the catchment area and beyond, but the school has local community responsibilities through hiring premises, for example for the choral society and some sporting activities. The school is situated in an area with an ageing population and is seen as a stable element and expected to retain traditional approaches. Opportunities for greater community involvement are, however, limited by the intensive use of premises by an 'over-full school with much accommodation which is too small for the groups who have to use it'. Active planning for a sports hall, sponsored by the PTA will, it is hoped, result in greater community involvement.

The impact of community expectations on professional development means staff are aware of the importance of continuing good exam results. Further, developing 'skills and knowledge within a subject area is most important'. However, the whole staff considers that, as a comprehensive, the school has to be able to enhance the opportunities for all its pupils and the recent emphasis has been on developing supportive work for pupils with learning difficulties, on matters of differentiation, and on teaching and learning styles appropriate to the spread of ability.

This is particularly important at 'sixth form level… we've had a tendency to spoon-feed them too much further down the school and, as a result, they find self-study a bit more than they can cope with!' This recognition is based on a growing awareness of the effects of pupil grouping upon achievement and a strengthened pastoral support system. A whole-school emphasis on teaching and learning has thus become linked to developing personal achievement and individual responsibility through personal and social education and an evolving report system.

The school became grant maintained two years ago as a result of 'the domino effect and the need for us to retain some funding during a period of declining LEA support', resulting in an 'increase in freedom to purchase the help we need from a wider area and a more diffuse network'. The management structure of the school is based on a senior management team with a head and three deputies with defined responsibilities for teaching and learning, personnel and staff development, and curriculum and timetable planning. Responsibility for professional development rests with the personnel deputy, while a colleague holding a major allowance is responsible for initial teacher education (ITE). Policy and planning is undertaken by the personnel deputy working with a Staff Development Committee of six staff drawn from all levels of experience. The teacher responsible for ITE is vice-chair of the committee, thus ensuring coordination of staff development and ITE opportunities.

The personnel deputy manages the budget for professional development activities but arrangements for cover are undertaken by a senior teacher. The professional development Special Purposes Grant (SPG) is split between several budget headings within the framework of 'development' and about one-third of the total is available for direct professional development work including a sum devolved to heads of department for their annual programmes. While there is a governors' personnel committee, its impact on professional development opportunities is limited.

Planning and Practicalities

The basic criteria against which all professional development activities are planned is the school development plan. This is the first year that a full and 'bottom-up' planning process is being used, which includes programming, costing and evaluation for all aspects of individual, departmental and whole-school development. It is thought, however, that there has been a shift of emphasis: all the staff were surveyed on their perceived development needs and this has been used to increase personal and departmental effectiveness. The evaluation of all SDP plans is based, in part, on assessments of the impact of developments on teaching and learning and subsequent pupil experiences. This leads to increased integration in classroom activity, the use of appropriate resources and the help given to staff in identifying appropriate development opportunities.

The process begins with departments or staff responsible for elements of the programme completing an annual submission of training needs at whole-school and departmental levels. Senior management and the Staff Development Committee then consider these before submitting a proposed programme to governors for approval. Priorities identified during this process become the criteria for subsequent professional development requests, but the personnel deputy is also anxious to meet targets which may be identified by individuals after their final appraisal interview, if appraisees are willing for these to be passed on.

The focus of whole-school inservice work is the annual autumn staff conference which uses two of the training days and aims to maintain whole-school themes and offer a diversity of workshops which build on departmental and other organizational group requests placed before the staff development committee. A menu of some 20 suggestions is offered to staff to ascertain the level of interest. The response to this forms the basis of a programme and each individual selects four workshops. Staff see this as offering choice, which enables decisions to be based on the way new skills or ideas can be used in departments – but also meet personal needs. Much of the workshop activity is organized by members of staff who have been involved in pilot work, such as the use of information technology.

Further development of this approach is helped by maintaining full evaluations of all activities which are considered in a post-mortem Staff Development Committee session. The status of activities is enhanced by automatic recording of attendance on each individual's record of professional development. Workshop quality 'is variable, but we often use colleagues as leaders and they're more likely to know what we need, and the level overall is good or better'. The need for a 'skilled link between the major themes and the actual workshops is the essence of a good programme'.

Consultancy is also fundamental to the autumn conference and to the help given to the equivalent of one and one-half days used by each department. A further half-day is allowed for pastoral group meetings. Until 1995, departmental and pastoral meetings included the option of one residential day alongside twilight sessions, but financial constraints may well affect the availability of residential facilities in future. Each department has a devolved budget for CPD but they often rely on school or subject networks to determine speaker and consultant quality. The deputy head maintains a careful record of outside contributions to activities and is currently evolving a more detailed evaluation system for this and all other external courses being used. This will 'help us to know what's available, to know how to balance reputation and cost, and to get what we need through responsiveness to our requests'. Whole-school issues evolved from senior management discussions are highlighted as themes for the year during meetings on the first day of the autumn term.

External courses may be undertaken at departmental or personal behest or where the SMT know that skills or information are needed for whole-school purposes, such as in an aspect of special needs. Individual professional development is helped by using record sheets for the autumn conference and the record of departmental needs. It is formalized in the initial induction of staff with additional sessions for newly qualified staff during their first year, organized in a network with other area schools. These sessions are seen to be 'helpful because we get to meet others in the same subject area and we concentrate on teaching and learning rather than on the protocol of the school which is an internal matter'.

All staff are free to submit their appraisal targets and a statement of their personal professional needs to the personnel deputy. A small fund exists to assist two or three staff each year to attend further courses, usually leading to a higher degree, at a university or college of higher education of their choice. Evaluation may be rather 'hit and miss on some courses, but we always report back to the deputy head and the other staff of the department... the reporting back may well be informal when you think of the number of staff who might be interested, but it's up to us to let others know whether things were worthwhile, and much more importantly, what the course did for us in getting knowledge or skills that we need'.

Attending subject-based courses and moderation meetings organized by examination boards is seen to be effective and directly related to the aims of the school. There is some concern that LEA offers from the county and two neighbouring authorities, while widely circulated, arrive too late to be 'of any use in planning what we want to do as a department – but individual teachers could be released at a late stage if all the administrative hurdles can be jumped'.

Beyond this, offers of courses 'are numerous... they come in and then they are sorted and distributed according to what is known of departmental and individual needs... the need for some form of quality assurance or registration becomes more evident. We don't know many of the providers and know even less of the actual presenters who might be used'. There is some concern that even courses and consultancies provided by high-profile organizations may not 'give what the school wants if they are not prepared to listen to our needs or to go through the planning stage with us'.

As a GM school the opportunity of using courses and consultancy from a wider field is appreciated by staff, but there is some regret 'that the quality of local LEA staff has deteriorated as they have had to put their resources into OFSTED work, because we knew who they were and what they could offer'. At the same time many regret losing a 'full local programme which could be used as a catalyst for individual interest... when a person saw something which he or she might not otherwise have thought about'.

The school's ITE policy is overseen by the deputy head responsible for teaching and learning. However, a close working relationship exists with the personnel deputy, and mentoring opportunities are negotiated at departmental level with the heads of department aware of individual professional growth needs. Decisions may, however, 'be affected by the need to timetable staff with particular groups and yet balance things in such a way that mentors have two periods a week for the work – the person most suited to, or most needing the experience, may not be the one who can be released in a particular timetable pattern'. This is seen as an example of the way in which 'ideals may be compromised and the needs of departments and individuals are balanced according to the overwhelming need to provide the best possible experience for the children.'

The Impact

The school development plan drives professional development. It has implications for the whole-school, the department and for individual staff, and efforts are made to reconcile all sets of objectives through the aim of improving teaching and learning. Staff acknowledge that the SDP is increasingly 'recognizing grass-roots opinion' and needs and this is having a knock-on effect in staff expectations regarding their own development process: 'we are becoming more proactive rather than reactive to outside influences... autumn conferences are encouraging us to be more assertive as we gain the confidence'.

The importance of heads of department in supporting and facilitating development is seen in departmental programmes and how meeting time is used. One department has a monthly topic-based development meeting and uses development 'along the way' through curriculum development planning and providing timetable allocation opportunities which extend and challenge staff. It is evident that staff contribute to planning at this level, but some feel they are only beginning to make an individual contribution to the whole-school programme.

Whole-school and departmental-level patterns of expenditure are not widely published, but it is accepted that 'this allows flexibility in responding to a changing scene' and staff are able to comment on efforts to meet needs. The close working relationship of departmental staff adds to opportunities 'for us to plan what we're going to do over our coffee... it's the sort of school where we help each other and discuss the needs we share'. Staff are aware of accreditation opportunities for school-based development in some areas and argue that, in a competitive situation, some way has to be found to gain further qualifications.

While appraisal is valued, it is as yet formally isolated from the development planning process. This may be because individual targets are only available for staff development if appraisees request it, or because appraisers are unaware of the importance of development needs and concentrate instead 'on matters like the allocation of work and the more effective teaching and learning in the classroom'. There are also problems of identification where an appraiser is not the head of department concerned. Some staff believe that if observation notes and targets were more widely available there would be a more immediate link to professional growth. The process and uses of appraisal are under review.

Departmental heads and individual staff are aware of the balance which needs to be struck between attending a course and the disruption to pupils. The dilemma is removed in some departments by the availability of a core team of supply staff who know the department and the school's ethos and are able to respond accordingly. The greater dilemma for individual teachers is that a course, say on middle management competence development, might not be immediately useful to the school, but is really required before promotion.

Identifying such dilemmas indicates that staff are becoming more aware of their needs and their expectations are that these should be met if they enhance the quality of teaching and learning. Overall, the attitude to professional development is positive, with staff recognizing that INSET days, course attendance and subject- or pastoral-based programmes have much to offer: 'the picture is one of declining cynicism about the use of precious time for further training'. The cost of this is seen to be 'in the need to find courses which are capable of providing what we need and which won't cause disruption by the need to travel long distances – only to find that what we get is of inferior quality'.

The importance of evaluation and dissemination within the school is recognized as 'the key to getting a system which gives us what we need... the move must be towards the school-centred provision rather than off-site courses'. Budget expenditure is interpreted widely to allow for a variety of development. However, staff expectations mean that the basic scheme currently offered is fundamental to their continuing capacity to effect change within and beyond their subject areas. The anxiety is that heightened individual expectations may not be met, either because teaching and learning priorities are dominant within a restricted budget, or because mapping needs and evaluating opportunities is a complex process. Current administrative changes in evaluation, information handling and establishing priorities may facilitate a closer tie between whole-school, departmental and individual needs.

CHAPTER 7

Towards Coherence in Professional Development

The case studies outlined in the previous chapter offer a variety of perspectives on the organization and purposes of professional development. This chapter seeks to bring together various strands explored in the case studies and in earlier chapters in order to propose possible strategies and a framework for achieving more coherent and workable professional development policies and practices in schools and colleges. Both survey and case study evidence highlight three particular aspects of continuing professional development:

1. the nature of the learning process;
2. the organization of CPD activities; and
3. the assimilation of development and training activities into individual, group, and institutional practice.

We begin by examining the experience of schools who have travelled along the road towards a more systematic and open approach to integrating professional development planning with school development planning as a support for establishing greater school effectiveness and improvement. Their experience suggests that, when a discernible and positive professional development culture exists which emphasizes professional growth, other targets also become attainable.

The Learning Process

Staff responding to the survey questionnaire identified a need for professional growth through reflection on practice and the development of thinking as well as practical skills. All learning is, however, a combination of knowledge, skills and attitude development Teaching staff and managers outlined activities which they saw as significant in supporting their own personal professional development. For example, 'one-off' courses and conferences initially provided 'opportunities to highlight specific topics' which in turn, framed 'more substantial CPD work', supported further skills development and was a stimulus for sharing specific knowledge, information and ideas. In addition, various CPD activities are perceived to have a multi-level impact – on individuals, working groups and/or on the whole-school. While long-term funded developments (eg, award-bearing courses and secondments) are far less widely available nowadays because of funding constraints, interviewees argue that schools can provide valuable learning venues and offer stimulating learning opportunities, provided reflection, review and planning are available, so that 'work' and 'development' may be more integrated in future.

Joyce and Showers (1980) identify the progression from awareness to competence. In their view, the training process should match objectives to a cycle of presentation, modelling, practice, feedback and necessary coaching to achieve the key objectives: essentially offering a skills-based approach. If this conception is accepted, CPD planners need to offer opportunities based on the appropriate learning level and link this with activities outlined in the cycle.

However, this approach is little more than part of what Miles (1986) describes as the initiation and implementation phases within the change process. Fullan (1991) also stresses the need to change the organizational culture rather than simply to attack individual elements of a programme. He argues that change can only occur through strategically planned activity which has an institutional dimension. In order to establish this, he suggests that individual aspects need to be much better integrated to create greater institutional awareness of what is being undertaken, and for what purposes. One teacher working in a case study school where staff are encouraged to develop their own learning programmes asserts that 'all life actually becomes a learning process – and if you think about what you do, whether its formal or informal, so much of our life in school really becomes professional development'.

The progression from skills-training to professional development is seen by numerous staff as a potentially significant gain from the appraisal process. Where appraisal targets and school development plan objectives are clearly related, openly published and evaluated, the prospects for changing the institutional culture appear to be much better. Recognizing the validity of this, Leithwood (1992) proposes a progression of competence in educational practice to the point where teachers' instructional expertise is first enhanced, then fosters growth in others and eventually includes participation in a broad array of whole-school decision-making which goes beyond subject-area confines. Box 7.1 offers a vignette based around the way in which one case study school managed change so that a number of staff felt that they had achieved a higher level of capability through professional development.

Box 7.1: Red Valley High School

In Red Valley School, the head and governing body have become aware that, while it is a pleasant and happy institution, it has consistently achieved only 'what's possible' for students and has not been making sufficient demands of either staff or students to maximize their potential to reach 'what's desirable' – and get the best possible results.

After attending a course on TQM, the head recognized that more could be achieved, provided the school saw the issue as a whole-community objective. Working parties, departmental meetings, meetings with members of the community (including parents and community groups at large), individual student interviews, and surveys of student, staff and parent attitudes all provided subjective opinions and ideas, as well as objective data which could be used as a starting point in discussion. Problem-solving sessions involved all groups in the school, facilitated by a consultant. Both LEA and HEI 'critical friends' were used as catalysts for discussion and subsequent action planning, with the aim of establishing a two-year action plan which would be acceptable to all sections within the school.

Senior staff acknowledged that staff attitudes needed to change, since 'there were those who said it couldn't be done'. The passage of time allowed several new key appointments to be made of people prepared to 'cajole and convince' others so that 'it might be done'. Two major staff conferences considered the 'inescapable' practical and philosophical changes, and an agreed plan embraced personal, departmental, year and whole-staff development priorities for the coming two years.

Above all, practical and attainable targets were set, for example attendance rates for parents' evenings, a reduction in student disruption, the establishment of measures for increased student self-esteem, and finally an improvement of 15 per cent in GCSE higher-grade passes. These were agreed as goals for all sections of the school. Two years later all targets had been more than met, but in the words of the headteacher, 'it has meant that as a staff we now think improvement and, more than that, we talk about it!'

In your experience...

Do the changes at Red Valley High School appear to be examples of well-managed innovation? How far is it an example of top-down or bottom-up change... or is it a combination of both? What would you list as the inhibiting and favouring factors for changes in your organization? What would most be needed from you and your colleagues?

A lack of shared values is likely to hinder developments in any organization, particularly where staff regard change as a threat to their established roles, practices or attitudes. For example, tensions within many staffrooms during comprehensive reorganization in the 1960s and 1970s and subsequent amalgamations to cope with falling rolls have left scars on professional relationships over a long period. The ability to manage micropolitical pressures (Hoyle, 1989) remains a necessary requirement for successful change, and work undertaken by Hopkins (1987) and developed through the International School Improvement Project (ISIP) demonstrates the importance of using staff and organizational development strategies which attempt to overcome these problems by creating simultaneous 'top-down/bottom-up' approaches to change.

This characterizes the way in which Red Valley School managed its development strategy: although senior managers outlined the principles which framed previously agreed aims, it was the teaching staff as a whole who ultimately undertook the necessary actions to establish effective change. It was they who established their own priorities, set their own targets and ultimately implemented changes. Nevertheless, a teacher in one KEEP project school strikes a cautionary note by suggesting that such a process is 'one which we could undertake for only a short time... it would be too difficult to sustain that kind of effort year after year because we really need time to take stock'.

Wallace (1991) shows that schools and colleges involved in managing complex initiatives since the 1988 Education Act, have needed to ensure these are prioritized, phased and planned. In several of our case study schools, the dangers in attempting to deal simultaneously with a plethora of activities is evidenced in the adverse comments of a number of teachers who feel they are being unfairly pressurized to attend 'quick burst' courses and to participate in SMT-driven training – which they feel may too often be detrimental to their main teaching task.

Interviewees also frequently comment that although professional development is an apparently proactive aspect of their professional lives, they are too often denied 'the opportunity to sit back and think' and reflect on key issues because of their pressurized workload. Kinder *et al.*'s (1991) analysis of training day activities notes how such occasions often consist of relatively low-order information-giving sessions: while immediate needs may be met, such training is neither particularly well received by participants nor has much impact on school development. It is possible that this research is now dated because much of the information-giving required for the introduction of the National Curriculum is completed, and the value of structured reflective activities is more widely appreciated. Nevertheless, 'drawer-tidying time' still belittles CPD in some institutions.

Increasingly, the pedagogy of professional development is geared to the needs of reflective and reflexive activity. The former may be analytic in quality, the latter uses this analysis to inform future action. Schon (1983) suggests that training focused on effective professional growth differs from that focused on repetitive, skills-based work. Duignan (1989) extends this idea to the leadership role in professional management, suggesting that personal reflection on experience leads to the development of a 'vocabulary' of responses and that these are based on an attempt to conceptualize professional activity. When faced with a similar situation the appropriate response is then used as a professional reaction.

Within classrooms, reflexive action builds on reflection as approaches associated with successful teaching become part of an individual's way of working. A number of teachers in our research project schools have suggested that this approach is developed through 'activities which give us a chance to think about what we do and why we do it... and the opportunity to talk to others so that we might gain from what they do'.

One problem is the difficulty of convincing those managing and organizing professional development that 'unstructured' time may be an appropriate INSET option within personal, departmental or even whole-school programmes.

The TTA's recent focus on how schools use their five 'training' days re-emphasizes the government's ongoing concern with accounting for professional development time. Because unstructured activities are not easily recorded or evaluated by outside agencies and require self-validation, the possibilities for continuing to allocate such time may remain limited. Despite this, one survey school encourages all staff to plan for one day a year – either within inservice days or by negotiation when their timetable is lighter – for an activity which specifically allows them 'time to think'.

While the range of potential activities is considerable, the professional morality amongst teachers is such that when offered unstructured 'development space' most tend to choose a subject-focused day with staff at a local HEI, work-shadowing, some form of industrial experience, or visits to another school. Too often they feel that 'people like to see that you're doing your job' and that it is implicitly frowned upon 'to take time to reflect'. For example, in one school with 29 staff, only three admit to taking time to 'think about what I do'. However, school-based action research as part of extended professional courses is seen as providing staff with alternative, more structured opportunities to reflect on the practical applications of research within their own working environment – something many value highly. This approach also appears to be seen as a useful way of offering 'reflective practitioners' greater professional credibility, as well as credentials!

Clearly, learning objectives for staff at various career stages will differ and there is growing evidence that PDCs are taking both 'age' and 'stage' into account when discussing development opportunities (Morant, 1981). For example, teachers asked to outline their sequence of needs tend to move from a skills-based foundation induction and early teaching experience, through to a competence focus, then on to the point where reflection-on-action enables them to examine and re-examine ways in which teaching is undertaken in different situations using alternative strategies. Finally, they move on to a conceptualization of practice and management of the teaching and learning environment (Liston and Leichner, 1987).

Interviewees' comments also showed that both teachers and managers may perceive themselves as moving through a 'professional journey'. This conceptualization influences the way they identify their professional development needs at any given moment, as one interviewee's 'journey' demonstrates in Box 7.2.

Box 7.2 A professional journey

Jane was typical of a number of teachers who...

'...started off with a need to get on top of my teaching skills generally and ideas about the way in which I could become a more effective home economics teacher... but as time's gone on I've been much more interested in managing... organizing learning and developing resources in my subject. So... actually I've done fewer courses and conferences over the last couple of years.

'Now, though, I'm much more interested in working with other teachers – my colleagues... and with being part of the team at school. I think I've gained most from doing the mentor training... in fact the year that I had working with our new staff has made me realize recently that, really, I'd like to know a lot more about the ways I can help... about how I can contribute to the school as a whole... and I'm finding that I increasingly want to look at how other people in other schools look at their – similar – roles... really, for me, it's now a matter of grabbing every opportunity I can get to have a bit of time – really to think – review things... either on my own or to go through things with other people... teachers and colleagues.'

In your experience...

Can you identify any pattern or progression in the way that you have been approaching your own professional development as part of your own career development – is your focus different now compared with an earlier stage?

It may be that, in your own case, you can identify a similar pattern developing to that followed by Jane although, as one headteacher in the research project commented, anyone developing a professional and career focus is likely to be strongly influenced by the balance between their subject interest and their general educational interest, and by their own individual involvement within the school – through, for example, membership of departmental or cross-curricular teams, as well as their part in whole-school groupings.

Within Europe more generally, teachers and senior managers tend to have more limited experience of whole-school professional development. In different countries this varies between one and nine days a year. Such days may focus predominantly on information transmission and skills enhancement; beyond this, any further training and development tends to be left to each individual's discretion. More substantial additional INSET provision is also usually targeted at primary and general secondary school teachers, rather than at specialist subject teachers in upper schools. While continuing professional development has been somewhat instrumental in the past, several European governments have more recently begun to establish new policy initiatives (see Box 7.3).

Box 7.3: European policy initiatives in CPD

Belgium (French sector)
Attempt to establish common aims, procedures and methods for all target groups.

Belgium (Flemish sector)
Individual schools to learn to identify their own needs.

Denmark
Increase in the ability of teachers to learn within a whole-school situation.

Greece
Additional opportunities to meet any gaps in teachers' knowledge and to match their broadening role.

France
Meeting the needs of the new working contract which broadens functions, structures and curriculum in secondary schools.

The Netherlands
School-based training to meet the needs of nationally prioritized under-privileged groups.

Portugal
Development of training which is directly relevant to classroom activity.

(Pepin, 1995)

These targets indicate the shifting focus towards teachers dealing with their own perceived developmental needs: any analysis of inservice experience is likely, therefore, to have a strong learning dimension which stresses personal as well as institutional benefits.

A key feature in the learning process is the ability to develop an accurate picture of the valuable ingredients within a learning experience, so that it can then form a basis for future review and action. Table 7.1 offers one way of identifying and recording how far an INSET activity or a period of development has been valuable as a learning experience. The table has several potential uses, eg, in assessing staff views of a single event; for assessing the learning experiences of an individual over time; or in helping to review expertise within a specific area as part of needs identification. Further, by aggregating all the staff responses within a specific department – or even within an institution – the table could prove useful as a way of developing an evidence base for both evaluation and planning purposes.

Table 7.1 is based on a hierarchy of descriptors and can be altered to reflect different qualities according to focus and need. Where the table is used to collect data, each of the appropriate descriptors can be ringed so that a profile can then be constructed.

While a potentially useful approach, it is also essential that we acknowledge its limitations. Learning experiences are clearly a great deal more than the sum of the various elements identified in this matrix and it is too simplistic to suggest that it offers a complete or exhaustive picture. Rather, it provides an organized starting point for development. Furthermore, such a matrix may be inappropriate for certain learning experiences, like induction, work shadowing or reflection, since these are clearly not amenable to such a schematic evaluation structure.

Table 7.1 *CPD experiences and the learning process: using descriptors to create an outline profile*

	Positive		Neutral		Negative
Knowledge	Enhanced; at a new level	More than anticipated	Increase as expected	Limited new knowledge	No new knowledge
Skills	Competent and confident	Competent	Improvement	Limited skills improvement	No new skills
Attitude	Strong change in thinking and action	Change in understanding and action	Change in understanding	Limited new understanding	No new understanding
Relevance	Highly relevant; opened new horizons	More than anticipated	Appropriate	Limited relevance	Not relevant at all
Stimulation/ focus on change	Very stimulating; enthusiastic for change	See potential in change	Worthwhile: some impact	Some enjoyment	No enjoyment, boring

Key Organizational Elements for Effective CPD

Although managing and coordinating professional development is a complex and potentially time-consuming process, it is also an important one, since organizational arrangements impact on and may well modify the effectiveness of the INSET learning process. Amongst what might be called the 'organizational inhibitors' to INSET which teachers pointed to as principal causes of dissatisfaction, they list inadequate time, poor accommodation, travelling distances to venues, inadequate funding, anxiety over supply staff arrangements and the backlog of work on return.

The success of professional development activities is often influenced by the degree to which they can be integrated into an institution's life, so that the learning process is enhanced by having optimum environmental and resource support. Lyons (1976) has argued that INSET provision tends to be either 'peripheral' (ie, ad hoc) or 'integral' (ie, more coordinated) to institutional life, while Kieviet (1990), writing within The Netherlands, has summarized the 'bottlenecks in inservice education' which, he argues, include inefficient and ineffective organization, a poor understanding of the design and organization of large-scale projects, poorly prepared presenters, and an overall failure to acknowledge the value of professional development within other work in the school.

Reflection...

Do you feel that CPD in your own school or college could be described as 'integral' or 'peripheral'? What kinds of external changes might facilitate better internal management of professional development within your own organization?

It may be that your own institution is part-way along the continuum between ad hoc and coordinated provision, with some aspects being more coherent that others. Within the UK, external limitations on INSET effectiveness are often connected with low funding levels and the range of legal requirements or constraints on the education service. Despite these limitations, however, delegated funding in the UK has allowed schools to become more autonomous decision-makers in specific areas. Within several European countries, including Spain, Luxembourg and Italy, centralized decision-making alongside tightly controlled supply staff arrangements and administratively determined programmes has effectively inhibited the establishment of school-based provision.

Evaluations of case study school policies and practices as well as discussions with a cross-section of staff in each of the project schools has enabled us to identify the following five organizational elements as a contribution to developing a framework for understanding professional development organization:

1. *information* (ie, the opportunities available);
2. *planning* (ie, decision-making);
3. *resources* (ie, funding and time);
4. *evaluation* (ie, the impact on teaching); and
5. *networks* (ie, available collegial and group opportunities).

Information

Interviewees' comments focused around three aspects of information and communication between providers and clients, as well as between colleagues within the client organization. There is, first, concern over the management and distribution of information produced externally, with a particular focus on the nature, appropriateness and impact of publicity material used by providers. Second, staff feel that the in-house management of information is highly variable and third, there is concern about the impact of information and publicity on the INSET market generally and institutional reputations.

The management of externally produced information was particularly criticized because publicity material from all external sources tended to 'arrive in a random way and to be highly variable in content'. There were also frequent comments about the timing and manner in which provider publicity was disseminated: both LEAs and independent agencies tend to publish material too late for effective programme planning within schools. In addition, publicity too often failed to give sufficient detail of content and approaches so that informed choices could be made: 'sometimes you get the feeling it's all a bit of a lottery.'

HEI information was generally regarded as being provided well in advance of events and courses, but was, nevertheless, criticized because, too often, it tended 'to rely on tried and trusted themes without recognizing the pace of change we have to face'. One teacher commented that even 'well-known speakers are of limited value if they only have the same message each time'.

The in-house management of information was also regarded as being variable in quality. It ranged from being highly systematic in some schools to random in others, with the effect that it brought frustrations over time wasted and difficulties over matching needs with available resources. A key challenge is to balance the need between making information openly available to staff while ensuring that it is drawn to the attention of key individuals responsible for group or personal opportunities. For example, several case study schools direct all incoming 'development' post to their PDC, who maintains a staffroom CPD noticeboard and notifies individual staff of forthcoming opportunities. In one school, the PDC then identifies how information links with known appraisal targets and highlights appropriate options at a staff briefing each week.

Finally, it was felt that insufficient attention was paid to the reputation of providers who now operate within 'a system where there is very little quality assurance and where professional development coordinators are seeking to plug gaps with whatever might be available'.

Planning

Planning issues created significant frustrations for those managing professional development. Both senior managers and PDCs strongly emphasized the need to improve opportunities for long-term planning, since 'at the moment it's all looked at on the short term', it 'makes impossible demands' and it 'requires us to know in February of year one which course we'll need to undertake in the summer term of year two… crazy!' The difficulties of balancing formal structures and spontaneous responses are also noted by PDCs. Despite this, there is also anxiety that attempts to plan completely for professional development activities – to include costings, venues, activity outlines, success criteria and evaluative procedures, etc. – will become overly restrictive, since 'the demands of rational planning preclude the flexibility to meet needs which may arise during the course of the year, as we work through new programmes of work or undertake new assessment procedures'.

Comments frequently point to a developing tension between using whole-school CPD events as a way of moving forward on a particular line of development, and meeting the needs of individuals and groups. Even attempts to allocate resources to specific sectors to achieve a fairer, more workable balance has sometimes been problematic, especially when specific groups have particular, high-cost or immediate needs. Increasingly, professional development committees in schools are beginning to adopt programme planning approaches, recognizing 'the need to integrate personal, group, and whole-school needs in a way which balances our resources with our requirements – with all our departments feeling they're being catered for'.

SDPs have been used in several project schools as agreed 'driving force' documents showing intentions and implementation strategies which have implications for professional development. However, not all recent developments have been entirely positive. Establishing personal targets through appraisal is producing a growing number of dissatisfied teachers who have established clearly identified development needs – especially in generic subject and management skills – which are not being met either wholly or partially as part of the school's programme. This is leading to a growing disenchantment or even cynicism with both the processes of and integration between appraisal and professional development as they currently operate. Earley (1995) points to this problem as 'a major stumbling block' in schools and also notes teachers' fears over 'having needs identified' through appraisal because 'it might be held against them at a later stage (for example, if or when, redundancies had to be made)'.

Reflection…

One respondent commented that 'all whole-school activity ensured departmental and individual development'. Do you think this is a possibility?

The difficulty with this view is that the required planning may be so complex that the benefits to be gained in CPD terms are potentially outweighed by the costs in other areas of management. Programme planning at departmental level may more easily produce integrated opportunities especially where departmental plans feed into whole-school programmes.

Resources

The wide variation in funding available for professional development constitutes a problem for schools, especially where the resource level is insufficient to support a reasonable proportion of both school and individual needs. Our research suggests that where schools are sufficiently well-funded, they devise carefully planned, imaginative and cost-effective programmes to enable them to support a full range of activities and staff, including shorter INSET, whole-school and in-house activities and some individual teacher support. This ability is, however, also dependent on the existence of effective management strategies and structures to support CPD.

The more minimal the funding, the greater the likelihood that schools will attempt to rely on their own home-spun programmes, with the emphasis resting predominantly on whole-school activities. As one PDC suggests, there are major difficulties faced by schools where 'the amount of money available has to be used in such a way that it supports activities which lead to a similar improvement in *all* areas of the school'.

Before budgets were devolved, many schools who had previously enjoyed high quality INSET provided by their LEA subject and advisory staff at no observable cost to their own budget, admit that they have found the process of adapting to greater autonomy has been difficult, especially where,

> the LEA agency still offers us the same people and we have the same expectations... but we now have to realize that they're on a different contract and they can't drop everything and come to us when our needs are greatest.

The adequacy of INSET funding also has to be matched against the concept of 'wise shopping' and there is growing evidence of considerable negotiation between schools and providers so that 'our funds are stretched according to who's available at the time... we look at alternative ways of doing things within our limits now rather than take the first idea we're offered'.

In effect, resource support for professional development can be analysed in terms of its adequacy, distribution, and knowledge of available options to achieve institutional development aims. In practical terms, the resource base also affects the availability of staff time to undertake activities, which in turn influences supply staff provision. While poorly funded schools minimize their use of supply staff, better endowed ones tend to utilize a staff replacement strategy or maintain smaller class sizes so that team teaching opportunities allow flexible teaching groups to be used to cope with staff absences. Whatever the effect of resource allocation it remains unclear whether patterns of class organization are substantially influenced by CPD in the UK. Arrangements in other parts of Europe illustrate alternative devices for managing staff absence and demonstrate the ways in which resource use for supply staffing is managed (see Box 7.4).

Box 7.4: Managing teacher replacement in Europe

Austria
Offers courses in term-time and the holiday periods. Attendance, while required to keep teachers up to date, is usually at the discretion of the teacher concerned and courses are limited to three days to contain the centrally funded costs. At the same time supply staff can only be used when staff have been absent for three days so the costs are minimized.

Greece
Offers permanently appointed teachers three months of up-dating training in regional centres once every five or six years throughout their teaching career. While the staff are absent their place is taken by a teacher undertaking initial training. Costs are centrally met.

Italy
Requires all teachers to devote 40 hours to inservice training either between 1 September and the start of the school year or between the end of classes and 1 June. Additional release is possible provided no further costs are incurred by using staff employed in the supply pool or those who are in schools where falling rolls have led to surplus staff.

Belgium
Within the French community two or three days each year are organized by the local inspectorate. Staff attending are not replaced and their pupils are given time off.

(Pepin, 1995)

In addition to examining the nature of information management, as well as planning and resources for professional development, we now consider two further elements which have an impact on the nature of effective INSET: evaluation and networking.

Evaluation

Evaluation for its own sake is clearly of limited value and is best used to secure future improvement through feedback to presenters and organizers, in addition to being made available to inform future development decision-making. While each of the case study schools acknowledges the need to evaluate, in some cases the process is being undertaken rather half-heartedly with only limited system back-up, application to single activities, or is left to the more conscientious individuals, departments or groups.

In addition, the nature of evaluation within schools seems to vary between brief, somewhat ad hoc, subjective and piecemeal commentaries – often noted in discussion either formally or informally – and the more structured record-keeping processes used to review INSET content, delivery and relevance which then contributes to annual (or sometimes termly) quality assurance reports and feedback.

The apparently close relationship between resource availability and the composition of development programmes also provides a further critical dimension. To some degree, evaluation requires a 'value-for-money' calculation to be undertaken. The comments of two senior managers are relevant here. One deputy head in a primary school notes that,

> there's no way that anything can have value for money if it gets in the way of effective classroom teaching – if we have to be absent then the kids lose and there's no value in that.

A secondary deputy head also argues that,

> the degree of disruption caused by professional development activities has got to be measured against benefits for our students, for pupils... really, though, the equation ought to be three-way – we *should* take into account the teacher, the taught and the future generations of youngsters who could gain.

Todd (1987), in a review of public service provision, suggests that the process of a 'practice audit' provides effective evaluation. His descriptors of the evaluation process include planning based on past experience in meeting needs; achieving aims through a balanced approach to individual and group learning; developing and using information; and using particular activities to guide future action-planning. Reviewing activities along these lines will, he argues, provide an effective cost-benefit analysis at an institutional level which can lead to enhanced collective review and planning.

Networks

The process of collective review shows the value of networking for groups and individuals. Teachers are increasingly anxious to establish and maintain their own networks to replace LEA networks which have seriously diminished with the decline in advisory support and teachers' centres. In spite of the difficulties, some LEAs have endeavoured to maintain a curriculum development focus in order to retain a professional and social ambience attractive to staff within their area. Dudley LEA, for example, maintains a development centre as a focus for investigative and development projects which also houses advisory staff able to provide incidental as well as formal support.

Professional associations and teacher unions represent another set of professional development networks which have sometimes been under-utilized in the UK over recent years, largely because of predominant concerns over conditions of service and major policy issues. More recently, however, unions have developed a higher development profile and networking impact, as the Secondary Heads Association 'roadshow' and its management development links with Oxford Brookes University show, emulating, in part at least, union involvement in staff development in British Columbia and Ontario, Canada.

Many school managers also feel that the initial focus of networks should be on 'similar professional and subject interests' which 'offer opportunities to reflect on the differing ways in which we do things', and that 'they should be relaxed enough to allow us to know each other rather than have to relate experiences in workshop style'. For effective professional development to take place, teachers argue that curriculum-focused meetings are a necessary first stage, with feedback offered to colleagues back at base afterwards.

The Organizational Environment for CPD

Taking up these five key organizational elements, we now consider a further set of descriptors which may be useful in building a specific picture of the professional development environment within an organization. Because the way CPD is managed and organized may impact on the nature of INSET experienced, the chance to audit the experience may prove a valuable review stage as part of an evaluation process. Using the five key environmental elements, each individual or group may use the matrix to build a picture of the development 'climate', showing how far CPD has been 'positive', 'neutral' or 'negative' in impact. Table 7.2 outlines a matrix structure and presents the range of possible environmental descriptors reflecting the way in which professional development is organized.

Table 7.2 *The organizational environment for professional development: some descriptors for the organization of CPD*

	Positive	Neutral			Negative
Information	Systematic and personalized	Systematic	Publicized on boards, etc	Randomly distributed	Available only on staff enquiry
Planning	PD planning tied to the IDP and balanced for individuals, group, staff	PD planning known and tied to SDP	PD allocated according to immediate needs	PD as requested	PD not part of a system
Resources	Allocated by need after discussion of IDP and appraisal	Delegated to departments and individuals	Allocated according to requests within annual limits	Allocated by senior staff without criteria	Subject to micro-political pressures
Evaluation	Records used for planning and value for money	Some use made of records for planning	System in place but records not used	Variable records	No formal system
Networks	Organized balanced opportunities	Encouraged but not systematic	Occasional opportunities to share views	Random pattern of contact	None

IDP: institutional development plan; PD: professional development

When trialled with a case study school, the matrix proved useful in assessing and categorizing individual staff perceptions of various aspects of CPD. For example, the PDC's role was perceived as more than merely facilitating development activities and opportunities, with staff feeling that the role demanded a broader view of the ways institutions could support the learning process. PDCs themselves feel they 'need to be fully involved with the planning team for the whole-school so that we can minimize communication problems'. In addition, it is vital that the PDC's role is seen as important by everybody 'so that we're not simply glorified administrators'. Many also felt they needed a greater input into programme planning for individual staff, not least 'because we know the difference between people genuinely seeking development and those who enjoy the diversion which some of our inservice brings with it'.

Undertaking a Professional Development Audit

The various organizational elements identified as contributing to the professional development environment and identified in Table 7.2 may be useful as a starting point for determining how far staff perceptions concerning CPD organization coincide with actual roles and responsibilities. Table 7.3 offers a structured and potentially useful way of determining the pattern and apparent efficiency of CPD management structures within an institution. By using Tables 7.2 and 7.3 in combination a more dynamic picture of the climate for effective professional development may be obtained.

Table 7.3 *A professional development audit: roles and responsibilities*

Name:	To meet individual need	To meet departmental need	To meet school need
Information provided by			
Planning prioritized by			
Resources allocated by			
Evaluation undertaken by			
Networking helped by			

For example, some schools have identified separate staff roles in order to cover a range of professional development functions. Impaired or complicated communication patterns between the key people responsible for the various aspects too often result in an unnecessary duplication of both provision and bureaucracy/paperwork, as well as a range of potentially unmet needs, particularly at departmental and individual levels.

If the names of individual staff responsible for various aspects of INSET are entered on the matrix in Table 7.3, a clearer picture of both the pattern and complexity of responsibilities emerges, showing where confused, poorly determined or multi-layered management responsibilities arise and where rationalization and role clarification may be appropriate. Where there is managerial and organizational coherence, it is likely that the same names of staff responsible for several linked aspects of development will occur in the columns. However, where no pattern can be detected or where a significant number of staff appear dotted throughout the matrix as responsible managers, the possibilities of confused management practices is increased and it is likely that there is less overall coherence in provision. Importantly, staff may find the situation even more confusing than the matrix shows. For example, where there are confused or blurred management responsibilities, the professional development climate is likely to be hazy and the issues of prioritizing, funding, delivery and the evaluation of professional development are usually overly complex.

In your experience...

Try using the audit matrix in Table 7.3 to investigate your own experience of INSET-related management. Does the process of audit highlight any problems inhibiting successful professional development within your own organization?

Your response may well show how far and in what ways professional roles and relationships are integrated within your institution. It may be that one person line-manages subject-based CPD, another has responsibilities for pastoral development, and yet another oversees appraisal-related development targets. Our evidence indicates that successful professional development appears to benefit from and requires an integrated rather than disconnected management approach, best facilitated by a more open and collegial professional ethos, where decision-making processes are clear to staff and where INSET is formally valued as part of the overall institutional culture.

Hutchinson's analysis (1993) of school development planning in a Northern Ireland primary school shows how effective planning requires 'orchestration' – a function of leadership which recognizes the strengths, resources, aspirations and the common culture of the school as the springboard for a leap forward. However, a cautionary note is also appropriate here: 'culture' is not a simple, readily grasped concept. Handy (1993) notes that it 'is a word sufficiently vague to cover all manner of specific approaches, but tends to connote inter-relationships, feedback mechanisms and appropriateness of fit', while Schein (1980) asserts that 'culture... is the assumptions which lie behind the values and which determine the behaviour patterns and the visible artefacts such as architecture, office layout, dress codes and so on'.

While the prevailing culture in an organization may mean that the majority of staff favour a particular line of development, a minority (or several minorities) may well feel antipathetic to specific developments or even to the general notion of changes in practice and custom. In addition, some individuals may wish, in the words of one interviewee, to 'plough their own development furrow' in a way which doesn't necessarily accord with the agreed institutional development plan. Each of these differing perspectives contributes to or detracts from the prevailing professional development culture and is bound to influence the overall integration and interaction of individual, department and whole-group activities.

Towards a Professional Development Culture

Sensitivity to these differing perceptions and a commitment to establishing clarity regarding roles provides a basis for, if not a solution to, reconciling differences of view. Following on from our earlier analysis, we would suggest that the nature of a professional development culture is complex and multi-faceted, involving several key elements, for example the nature of information flows and controls; the degree to which open planning exists; the strategies used for resource allocation to achieve aims; the ways in which evaluation forms a basis for review and development; and the ways in which networking facilitates mutual support and reflection.

While an environmental framework has been used elsewhere as a basis for classifying specific aspects of the school climate (Glover and Mardle, 1995), its use was specific and focused on mentoring for initial teacher training. The professional development matrix offered in Table 7.4 provides a more substantial and in-depth picture of the kinds of professional cultures within which valuable continuing professional development may (or may not) take place. It offers a graduated range of indicators and allows all staff to create a framework picture of the environmental structure in which CPD takes place. However, like all matrices it remains an analytical tool rather than a prescriptive template which purports to show how professional development 'ought' to operate. That remains a matter for individual institutions. The matrix offers a taxonomy identifying three kinds of situation:

1. *adverse cultures* – those which inhibit or even undermine any meaningful or significant professional development because they are randomized or unplanned and are unrelated to the overall organizational aims and objectives;
2. *neutral cultures* – those which, overall, neither inhibit nor enhance CPD, usually because it is often seen as comprising one-off and limited activities, the full significance of which is neither appreciated nor used; and

165

3. *supportive cultures* – those which enable staff to 'grow' professionally because their potential for achievement is released and the interaction between the key elements and development is recognized and encouraged.

Table 7.4 *Towards a professional development culture: a possible taxonomy*

	Individual	Department	Whole-school
Adverse	Random information; no encouragement to participate outside the school; appraisal targets ignored	Little coherence; information haphazard; resources allocated on a 'wait and see' basis, no networking; no regular evaluation	Multiple management of information; plans imposed rather than discussed; minimal participation by ordinary staff
Neutral	Policy of bidding to responsible Senior Manager on the basis of notices of courses; allocation on first-come-first-served system; evaluation by filed report; networking limited	Department holds information and makes it available if requested; tendency to be pragmatic in approach; little reporting back	Programme developed out of institution's development plan discussion but imposed on staff; resources 'bespoke'; limited evaluation of activities; no link to appraisal, etc
Supportive	Appraisal targets notified and related to the institutional development plan; funding to meet some development where possible, established networks	Departmental policies according to needs; funding made available for department use; networking and evaluation maintained; participative decision-making linked to whole-school and individual targets	Staff discussion establishes priorities; information sought, bids managed, resources allocated according to programme; thorough and published evaluation; networks established

Table 7.4 outlines the descriptors used in determining the nature of a professional development culture and links with and draws on concepts outlined in the preceding tables.

Few schools are likely to be viewed as adverse in all areas. It is more likely that individual experiences will vary significantly because personal aspirations may not accord with group or whole-school norms. The aggregated perceptions of individual colleagues may prove valuable indicators of overall staff views of school support and development mechanisms, providing a benchmark for the future enhancement of an organization's professional development culture. It might also indicate, for example, where specific departments or groups are working against – albeit unwittingly – generally agreed school practices. Finally, individual perceptions may give added force to the appraisal discussion process. In effect, findings derived from this type of investigation offer a straightforward and relatively structured way of initiating the evaluation of professional development. In doing so, they contribute to organizational review and planning processes.

In assessing professional development across Europe, some commentators have reviewed the importance of rationalizing provision so that supply and demand are more effectively harmonized (Pepin, 1995). The need to ensure that schools initiate changes in response to their own identified needs has also been emphasized, along with the importance of developing effective evaluation processes in relation to both the impact of INSET and the value added by providers. Some examples of these broader international concerns are given in Box 7.5.

Box 7.5: Room for rationalization? Professional development practices in Europe

Iceland
It often happens that the same teachers attend courses year after year while others seldom, if ever, appear. There is a danger that if only one or a very few teachers from a certain school attend an inservice training course, what they learn will fail to spread to others or will even be forgotten, resulting in little improvement to teaching in the school.... By ensuring the simultaneous participation and professional renewal of many teachers from the same school, the changes should be more effective. (p.192)

Greece
The gaps in teachers' knowledge, the ever changing requirements of the school curricula, and the tendency to broaden the teacher's role, form the basis for the organization and provision of the various training programmes. (p.78)

Denmark
In the inservice training of teachers at the general upper secondary level, priority is given to programmes in the schools themselves in which all teachers can participate at the same time and to 'monitoring' activities involving groups of teachers. (p. 58)

(Pepin, 1995)

The comments in Box 7.5 were prepared by senior inspectors in each country concerned and reflect the increasing focus on more systematic school improvement strategies where professional development is integrated with curriculum change. The need for appropriate funding, effective pedagogy and inclusive organization is also acknowledged. In England and Wales, the TTA estimates that £400 million is spent on professional development work annually (Pyke, 1995) although this figure includes teachers' salaries for their five professional development or training days, rather than simply grants and funds to support professional development. Regardless of the level of funding support, the amount of INSET funding available to each individual school and the way in which this is used, also show wide per capita variations.

Our research suggests that many schools need to establish a major shift in staff attitudes to professional development. The level of involvement, commitment and benefit varies so considerably that many institutions and individuals are currently inhibited from maximizing their potential – and thus failing to fully benefit students. One headteacher interviewee suggests that the key is 'to move our staff development system into our planning process so that it sits alongside our school development planning and ideas on improvement... then things will really change'.

There is a considerable degree of awareness amongst staff that too often 'things aren't working productively enough' at present. A cross-section of staff in several of the survey schools considered that too much professional development remains 'tacked on', especially where insufficient funds begin to inhibit programmes which have been patiently built on real staff needs and an identification of the best available support. In addition, some significant levels of cynicism still exist. Following a series of government-imposed changes, beginning with the teachers' pay disputes during the 1980s, a number of staff now regard professional development as largely instrumental, narrowly focused on 'squeezing more and more out of us' and too often targeted at information transfer, where the focus is most often focused on *training* rather than *development*.

Johnson (1992) suggests that while strategic change may be needed for effective development to occur, it is vital that an organization's cultural perspective also changes, particularly where collective ideas or beliefs are 'owned' by staff. Failure to address this issue may result in increasing resistance to change which ultimately places the institution at a disadvantage *vis-à-vis* its competitors and its pupils. While notions of competition are still anathema to many educationists, this issue is illustrated within some case study schools where the appointment of a new headteacher has been the catalyst which has encouraged and enabled existing teaching staff to re-examine their institution's 'competitive' position in the local education market.

While this is an initially difficult process, heads have noted that 'the link between change and future attractiveness is given much more push when the other link between enrolment and income is expressed in terms of possible redundancies'.

It may be, however, that this is not the only catalyst needed to encourage schools to pause to assess their present position and develop strategies for their future development. Where case study schools have evaluated their strategic position, they claim that a SWOT analysis (a whole-staff review of the organization's strengths, weaknesses, opportunities and threats) of its environment,

> focuses the mind and enables us to decide our four main objectives in future
> – improving teaching and learning, improving the environment, improving
> relationships with the community, and improving opportunities for everyone
> to give them confidence in the school's new role.

Our research shows that this approach was most successful where colleagues were given sufficient time to assess their own personal, group, and whole-school concerns in meeting each of the long-term targets. At the initial 'situational audit' stage, school staff assemble data showing 'where they're at' in relation to attaining their longer-term objectives. While this audit may take several forms, several schools have tried to identify, for example, how far appraisal and school evaluation have been able to provide relevant and stimulating development opportunities for both individuals and groups of staff within the school.

A number of senior management teams responding to our investigations outlined how, in their attempts at internal improvement strategies, they asked staff to identify areas with potential for further 'investigation' and encouraged the inclusion of both process improvements like 'better inservice days and more departmental curriculum planning meetings' in secondary schools and 'time to talk through developments with someone from outside who understands' in the primary sector, and *outcome targets* like 'improved homework completion' and 'improved reading fluency by KS 1'.

The focus on achieving agreed time-limited targets (however poorly defined initially) does at least provide a structure which enables colleagues to think through a range of alternative strategies and develop tactics to meet identified objectives. This strategy has proved effective in both secondary and primary schools, where National Curriculum demands have encouraged what might be called an 'in adversity tendency to collaborate', especially within subject groupings. One interviewee argues that the key element in professional growth is that it effectively enhances classroom practice because 'we haven't got the time to think too much about the higher ideals of education…

initial training rather failed us there... but we need to know how we can be most helpful to our youngsters'.

This suggests, perhaps, that staff needs might best be met not solely by providing more INSET courses, but by providing more time for planning, ideas development and materials development so that teaching is progressively enhanced. In effect, this means viewing teachers as professionals bent on self-improvement. There are times, however, when the most committed teachers may pursue poorly articulated analyses and poorly defined strategies, which limits progress. As one primary head comments: 'we need definite objectives which we're able to match against the success criteria we set ourselves so that, in the end, we can say, well, plan one worked, but plan two was much less successful'.

In effect, this means that teachers and schools need support and time to follow a cycle involving audit, planning, implementation and evaluation for each of the activities they pursue as part of their development strategy. The KEEP research suggests that 'reflection time' gets lost once plans begin to be implemented – potentially a crucial failing since,

> the fact that we go on from year to year trying to meet all these new demands
> overtakes our need to think about the water under the bridge... we're good
> at planning, but we're not so good on the review and restructuring!

If this is true of curriculum and policy changes within schools, it is also true of CPD policy development and programme planning. Reflection and review appear to be increasingly appreciated tools in the organizational development of schools, as well as important contributors to greater school effectiveness. However, it remains the case that evidence from both case study and survey schools suggests that review and restructuring opportunities too often remain limited, infrequently offered and consequently failing ultimately to meet enhanced expectations.

In institutions where a positive professional development culture exists, staff regularly review, enhance and change their roles. Where more conservative role-cultures predominate, opportunities for review are rare, enhancement is virtually non-existent and change becomes difficult to achieve. Reflecting a concern to meet the challenges presented by the cycle of audit, planning, implementation and review, one deputy head suggests that 'we need to see how professional development works in this place... how it meets what people want of it... and what it does to meet their needs'. We hope that some of the ideas outlined here may be useful in meeting that challenge.

References

Anderson, L (1991) 'Managing professional development in grant maintained schools', *Management in Education*, **5** (2), 7–8.

ap Thomas, J (1994) 'Mentors for staff development', *Management in Education*, **8** (2).

Archer, E G and Peck, B T (1991) *The Teaching Profession in Europe*, Glasgow: Jordanhill College of Education.

Audit Commission (1989) *Losing an Empire, Finding a Role: The LEA of the future*, London: The Audit Commission/HMSO.

Baker, K (1986) *LEA Responses to the New INSET Arrangements*, Slough: NFER.

Ball, S (1990) *Politics and Policy Making in Education: Explorations in policy sociology*, London: Routledge.

Bayne-Jardine, C and Holly, P (1994) *Developing Quality Schools*, London: Falmer Press.

Blackburn, V and Moisan, C (1987) *The Inservice Training of Teachers in the Twelve Member States of the European Community*, Education Policy Series, Maastricht: Presses Interuniversitaires Européenes.

Board of Education (1944) *Teachers and Youth Leaders. Report of the committee appointed by the President of the Board of Education to consider the supply, recruitment and training of teachers and youth leaders* (The McNair Report), London: HMSO.

Bolam, R (1982a) *Inservice Education and Training of Teachers: A condition for educational change*, Paris: OECD.

Bolam, R (ed.) (1982b) *School-focused Inservice Training*, Oxford: Heinemann.

Bolam, R (1993) 'Recent developments and emerging issues', in *The Continuing Professional Development of Teachers*, London: General Teaching Council for England and Wales.

Bradley, H and Howard, J (1992) 'Where are they now? The impact of long courses on teachers' careers and development', *British Journal of Inservice Education*, **18** (3), 186–90.

Briault, E (1976) 'A distributed system of educational administration', *International Review of Education*, London: Dent and Sons.

Burgess, R (1993) 'The context of In-service education and training', in Burgess *et al.*, *Implementing In-Service Education and Training*, London: Falmer Press.

Bush, T, Coleman, M and Glover, D (1994) *Managing Autonomous Schools*, London: Paul Chapman.

Busher, H (1990) 'Managing compulsory INSET under teachers' new conditions of service', *Educational Management and Administration*, **18** (3), 39–45.

Caldwell, B and Spinks, J (1988) *The Self Managing School*, London: Falmer Press.

CCCS (1981) *Unpopular Education*, London: Hutchinson.

Coombe, C and White, R (1994) 'Improving the management and professional leadership skills of school heads in Africa: A development model', *Studies in Educational Administration*, 60, Winter.

Copley, J and Thomas, D (1995) 'Comprehensively appraised', *Management in Education*, 9 (4), 7.

Darling-Hammond, L and Ascher, C (1992) *Creating Accountability in Big City Schools*, New York: NY ERIC Clearinghouse on Urban Education.

Darling-Hammond, L, Wise, A E, and Pease, S R (1986) 'Teacher evaluation in the organisational context: a review of the literature', in House, E R (ed.) *New Directions in Educational Evaluation*, London: Falmer Press.

Day, C (1989) 'INSET: the marginalising of higher education', *British Journal of Inservice Education*, 15, 195–6.

Dean, J (1993) *Professional Development in School*, Buckingham: Open University Press.

Department for Education (1993) *The Government's Proposals for the Reform of Initial Teacher Training*, London and Cardiff, DfE/Welsh Office.

Department of Education (1963) *Report of the Committee on Higher Education* (The Robbins Report), London: HMSO.

Department of Education, Employment and Training (1988) *Teachers Learning: Improving Australian Schools through In-service Teacher Training and Development*, Canberra: AGPS.

Department of Education and Science (1972a) *Teacher Education and Training* (The James Report), London: HMSO.

Department of Education and Science (1972b) *Education: A framework for expansion*, London: HMSO.

Department of Education and Science (1978) Advisory Committee on the Supply and Training of Teachers (ACSTT), *Making INSET Work*, London: HMSO.

Department of Education and Science (1984) Advisory Committee on the Supply and Education of Teachers (ACSET), *The In-Service Training and Professional Development of School Teachers*, Report of the Teacher Training Sub-Committee, London: HMSO.

Department of Education and Science (1985) *Better Schools* (White Paper), London: HMSO.

Department of Education and Science (1986) *Local Education Authority Training Grants Scheme*, Circular 6/86, London: HMSO.

Department of Education and Science (1990) *Developing School Management: The Way Ahead*, a report by the School Management Task Force, London: HMSO.

Department of Education and Science (1992) *Initial Teacher Training (Secondary Phase)*, Circular 9/92, London: HMSO.

Duignan, P (1989) 'Reflective management: the key to quality leadership', in Riches, C and Morgan, C (eds) *Human Resource Management in Education*, Buckingham: Open University Press.

Earley, P (1991) 'Defining and assessing school management competences', in *Management in Education*, 5 (4).

Earley, P (1992) *The School Management Competences Project*, Crawley: School Management South.

Earley, P (1995) *Managing our Greatest Resource: The Evaluation of the Continuous Professional Development in Schools Project*, London: NFER/UBI.

Earley, P and Fletcher-Campbell, F (1989) *Time to Manage*, Slough: NFER.

Easterby-Smith, M (1986) *Evaluation of Management Education, Training and Development*, Aldershot: Gower.

Ecclestone, K (1995) 'From NVQs to "policy scholarship": Evolving a research agenda for post-compulsory professional development', *British Journal of In-Service Education*, **21** (2), 117–35.

Education (1996) 'Suppliers take note of the marketplace', 5 January, p.2.

Elliott, B and MacLennan, D (1994) 'Education, modernity and neo-conservative school reform in Canada, Britain and the US', *British Journal of Sociology of Education*, **15** (2).

Elliott, J (1991a) 'Competency-based training and the education of the professions', in *Action Research for Educational Change*, Buckingham: Open University Press.

Elliott, J (1991b) *Action Research for Educational Change*, Buckingham: Open University Press.

Eraut, M (1993) 'The characterisation and development of professional expertise in school management and teaching', *Educational Management and Administration*, **21** (4).

Fielding, M (1996) 'The muddle in the middle', *Times Education Supplement*: School Management Update, 19 January, p.8.

Fisher, D, Grady, N and Fraser, B (1995) 'Associations between school-level and class-room-level environment', *International Studies in Educational Administration*, **23** (1), 1–15.

Fullan, M (1990) 'Staff development, innovation and institutional development', in Joyce, B (ed.) *Changing School Culture through Staff Development*, Alexandria, VA: Association for Supervision and Curriculum Development.

Fullan, M (1991) *The New Management of Educational Change*, London: Cassell.

Fullan, M (1992) *Successful School Improvement*, Buckingham: Open University Press.

Fullan, M (1993) *Change Forces: Probing the Depths of Educational Reform*, London: Falmer Press.

Fullan, M and Hargreaves, A (1992) *What's Worth Fighting for in your School?*, Buckingham: Open University Press.

Gealy, N (1993) 'Development of NVQs and SVQs at higher levels', *Competence and Assessment*, **21**, 4–10.

Gilroy, P and Day, C (1993) 'The erosion of INSET in England and Wales: Analysis and proposals for a redefinition', *Journal of Education for Teaching*, **19**, February.

Gleeson, D, Turrell, D and Russell, V (1994) 'Undertaking collaborative enquiry: evaluation for a change', in Bayne-Jardine, C and Holly, P (eds) *Developing Quality Schools*, London: Falmer Press.

Glover, D and Law, S (1995) 'Meeting needs… and developing processes', *Management in Education*, **9** (5).

Glover, D and Mardle, G (eds) (1995) *The Management of Mentoring*, London: Kogan Page.

Gow, L and McPherson, A (eds) (1980) *Tell Them from Me*, Aberdeen: Aberdeen University Press.

Green, H (1991) 'Assessment for senior management development', *Management in Education*, **5** (4).

Hall, V, Mackay, H and Morgan, C (1986) *Headteachers at Work*, Buckingham: Open University Press.

Halpin, D, Croll, P and Redman, K (1990) 'Teachers' perceptions of the effects of in-service education', *British Journal of Educational Research*, **16** (2), 163–77.

Hamlin, B (1990) 'The competent manager in secondary schools', *Educational Management and Administration*, **18** (3).

Handy, C (1993) *Understanding Organisations*, London: Penguin.

Harding, D (1995) 'Developing a development plan', *Management in Education*, **9** (4), 23.

Harding, R and Mann, P (1996) 'Anxiety about advice: a serious decline in specialist support to schools', *Education*, 5 January, p.7.

Hargreaves, D and Hopkins, D (1991) *The Empowered School*, London: Cassell.

Harland, J, Kinder, K and Keys, W (1993) *Restructuring INSET: Privatisation and its Alternatives*, Slough: NFER.

Harris, A, Jameson, I M and Russ, J (1995) 'A study of accelerating departments', *School Organisation*, **15** (3).

Hewton, E (1988) *School-focused Staff Development Guidelines for Policy Makers*, London: Falmer Press.

HMI (1977) *Ten Good Schools*, London: HMSO.

HMI (1993) *The Management and Provision of Inservice Training Funded by the Grant for Education and Support (GEST)*, a report from the office of Her Majesty's Chief Inspector of Schools, London: OFSTED.

Hopkins, D (ed.) (1987) *Improving the Quality of Schooling*, London: Falmer Press.

Hoyle, E (1989) 'The micropolitics of schools', in Bush, T (ed.) *Managing Education Theory and Practice*, Buckingham: Open University Press.

Hughes, M G (1972) 'The role of the secondary head', PhD thesis, University of Wales, cited in Hall, V, Mackay, H and Morgan, C, 'Headteachers at work: practice and policy', p.85, in Glatter, R *et al.* (1989) *Understanding School Management*, Buckingham: Open University Press.

Hutchinson, B (1993) 'The effective reflective school: visions and pipedreams in development planning', *Educational Management and Administration*, **21** (1), 4–17.

Johnson, G (1992) 'Managing strategic change: strategy, culture and action', *Long Range Planning*, **25** (1).

Joyce, B (ed) (1990) *Changing School Culture Through Staff Development*, Alexandria, VA: Association for Supervision and Curriculum Development.

Joyce, B (1991) 'The doors to school improvement', *Educational Leadership*, **48** (8).

Joyce, B and Showers, B (1980) 'Improving in-service training: the messages of research', *Educational Leadership*, **37** (5), 379–85.

Kerry, T (1993) 'Training days', *Management in Education*, **7** (1), 26–8.

Kieviet, F (1990) 'A decade of research on teacher education in the Netherlands', in Tisher, R and Wideen, M (eds) *Research in Teacher Education*, London: Falmer Press.

Kinder, K, Harland, J and Wootten, M (1991) *The Impact of School Focused INSET on Classroom Practice*, Slough: NFER.

Kirk, G (1988) *Teacher Education and Professional Development*, Edinburgh: Scottish Academic Press.

Knight, J (1992) 'The political economy of industrial relations in the Australian education industry (1987–1991)', *Unicorn*, **18**, 27–38, cited in Knight J, Bartlett, L and McWilliam, E (eds) (1993) *Unfinished Business: Reshaping the teacher education industry for the 1990s*, Queensland: University of Central Queensland.

Knight J, Lingard, R and Porter, R (1991) 'Re-forming the education industry through award restructuring and the new federalism?', *Unicorn*, **17** (3), 133–8.

Law, S and Glover, D (1993) *Changing Partners: Professional Development in Transition*, Keele University: Keele Professional Development Papers.

Law, S and Glover, D (1995) 'The Professional Development Business: School evaluations of LEA and higher education INSET provision', *British Journal of Inservice Education*, **21** (2), 181–92.

Law, S and Glover, D (1996) 'Mean, lean and local', *Times Educational Supplement*: School Management Update, 19 January, p.5.

Leclercq, J M 'Les structures administratives et pédagogiques des systemes éducatifs des pays de la Communauté européene: diversité and convergences, consequences sur la formation continuée des enseignants' (1988) (cited in Pepin, 1995, op. cit.).

Leithwood, K (1992) *Teacher Development and Educational Change*, London: Falmer Press.

Levacic, R and Glover, D (1994) *Efficiency and Effectiveness in Secondary School OFSTED Reports*, Buckingham: Open University.

Levacic, R and Glover, D (1995) *Measuring Efficiency and Effectiveness in Schools*, Milton Keynes: CEPAM, Open University.

Levin, B (1994) 'Improving educational productivity through focus on learners', *Studies in Educational Administration*, 60, Winter.

Liston, D and Leichner, M (1987) 'Reflective teacher education and moral deliberation', *Journal of Teacher Education*, **36** (8).

Litawski, R (1993) 'The "nappy and noses" brigade', *Times Educational Supplement*, 2 April, p.6.

Lyons, G (1976) *A Handbook of Secondary School Administration*, Slough: NFER.

McBurney, E and Hough, J (1989) 'Role perceptions of female deputy heads', *Educational Management and Administration*, **17**, 3, 115–18.

McCann, L (1994) 'Profiles and competences: ITT to NQT', *Management in Education*, **8** (2).

Maclure, M (1989) 'Anyone for INSET? Needs identification and personal/professional development', in McBride, R (ed.), *The In-service Training of Teachers*, London: Falmer Press.

McMichael, P, Draper, J and Gatherer, W (1995) 'Improving benefits and reducing costs: managing educational secondments', *Educational Management and Administration*, **23** (4), 245–53.

Miles, K (1986) *Research Findings on the Stages of School Improvement*, New York: Centre for Policy Research.

Montgomery, W (1990) 'Work shadowing', *Management in Education*, **4** (3), 21–3.

Morant, R (1981) *In-service Education within the School*, London: George Allen and Unwin.

Morris, G (1990) 'Towards the millennium', *Education*, 5 January, pp.9–10.

Murgatroyd, S and Morgan, C (1992) *Total Quality Management and the School*, Buckingham: Open University Press.

National Commission on Education (1993) *Learning to Succeed*, Report of the Paul Hamlyn Foundation, Oxford: Heinemann.

Neave, G (1992) *The Teaching Nation: Prospects for teachers in the European Community*, Oxford: Pergamon Press.

Oakland, J (1989) *Total Quality Management*, Oxford: Butterworth-Heinemann.

Oldroyd, D and Hall, V (1991) *Managing Staff Development: A handbook for secondary schools*, London: Paul Chapman.

O'Sullivan, F, Jones, K and Reid, K (1988) *Staff Development in Secondary Schools*, London: Hodder and Stoughton.

Ouston, J (1993) 'Management competences, school effectiveness and education management', *Education Management and Administration*, **21** (4).

Page, B and Fisher-Jones, L (1995) *Survey of Continuing Professional Development*, Research conducted for the Teacher Training Agency, London: MORI.

Pearce, J (1986) *Standards and the LEA*, Windsor: NFER Nelson.

Pepin, L (1995) *In-service Training of Teachers in the European Union and the EFTA/EAA Countries*, Brussels: EURYDICE.

Peters, T (1988) *Thriving on Chaos: Handbook for a management revolution*, London: Pan.

Peters, T and Waterman, R (1982) *In Search of Excellence*, London: Harper & Row.

Pfeffer, N and Coote, A (1991) *Is Quality Good for You? A critical review of quality assurance in the welfare services*, London: Institute of Public Policy Research.

Pyke, N (1995) 'Bid to dispel training gloom', *Times Educational Supplement*, 3 November, p.4.

Rae, K (1994) 'The challenge of tomorrow's schools', *Studies in Educational Administration*, 59, Summer, 33–40.

Sallis, E (1992) *Total Quality Management and Education*, London: Kogan Page.

Schein, E (1980) *Organisational Psychology*, London: Prentice Hall.

Schon, D (1983) *The Reflective Practitioner*, London: Harper-Collins.

Stacey, R (1992) *Managing the Unknowable*, San Francisco, CA: Jossey-Bass.

Stoll, L and Fink, D (1988) 'An effective schools project: the Halton approach', in Reynolds, D, Creemers, B and Peters, T (eds) *School Effectiveness and Improvement*, Wales: University of Wales College of Cardiff.

Thomas, M (1994) 'Going into business: an LEA's training menu', *Management in Education*, 8 (2).

Todd, F (1987) *Planning Continuing Professional Development*, Beckenham: Croom Helm.

Triggs, E and Francis, H (1990) *The Value of Long (Award-bearing) Course for Serving Teachers*, London: Institute of Education.

Trimble, A (1993) 'Managing a staff development policy in the primary school', *Management in Education*, 7 (2).

Veuglers, W and Zijlstra, H (1995) 'Learning together: In-service education in networks of schools', *British Journal of In-Service Education*, 21 (1), 37–47.

Walker, A and Scott, K (1993) 'The worth of senior management teams: some pointers to improvement', *Studies in Educational Administration*, 58, Winter.

Wallace, M (1991) 'Flexible planning: a key to the management of multiple innovations', in *Educational Management and Administration*, 19 (3), 180–93.

Wallace, M and Hall, V (1994) *Inside the SMT*, London: Paul Chapman.

Warwick, D (1975) *School-based In-Service Education*, London: Oliver and Boyd.

West-Burnham, J (1992) *Managing Quality in Schools*, Harlow: Longman.

Whitcombe, A (1992) 'Planning for quality – selecting success criteria', *Management in Education*, 6 (3), 13–15.

Whitty, G and Wilmott, E (1991) 'Competence-based teacher education: approaches and issues', *Cambridge Journal of Education*, 21 (3), 309–18.

Wideen, M and Holborn, P (1990) 'Teacher education in Canada: a research review', in Tisher, R and Wideen, M (eds) *Research in Teacher Education: International Perspectives*, London: Falmer Press.

Wilkin, M and Sankey, D (1994) *Collaboration and Transition in Initial Teacher Training*, London: Kogan Page.

Williams, M (1991) *In-Service Education and Training*, London: Cassell.

Index

Lightning Source UK Ltd.
Milton Keynes UK
13 May 2010

154094UK00003B/136/A